PTSD

Proven Psychological Techniques for Managing Trauma

(The Complete Guide to Understanding, Treating and Recovering From Trauma)

Wesley Smith

Published By **Bella Frost**

Wesley Smith

Ptsd: Proven Psychological Techniques for Managing Trauma (The Complete Guide to Understanding, Treating and Recovering From Trauma)

ISBN   978-1-998927-26-5

No part of this guidebook shall be reproduced in any form without permission in writing from the publisher except in the case of brief quotations embodied in critical articles or reviews.

Legal & Disclaimer

The information contained in this book is not designed to replace or take the place of any form of medicine or professional medical advice. The information in this book has been provided for educational & entertainment purposes only.

The information contained in this book has been compiled from sources deemed reliable, and it is accurate to the best of the Author's knowledge; however, the Author cannot guarantee its accuracy and validity and cannot be held liable for any errors or omissions. Changes are periodically made to this book. You must consult your doctor or get professional medical advice before using any of the suggested remedies, techniques, or information in this book.

Upon using the information contained in this book, you agree to hold harmless the Author from and against any damages, costs, and expenses, including any legal fees potentially resulting from the application of any of the information provided by this guide. This disclaimer applies to any damages or injury caused by the use and application, whether directly or indirectly, of any advice or information presented, whether for breach of contract, tort, negligence, personal injury, criminal intent, or under any other cause of action.

You agree to accept all risks of using the information presented inside this book. You need to consult a professional medical practitioner in order to ensure you are both able and healthy enough to participate in this program.

Table Of Contents

Chapter 1: What Is Post-Traumatic Stress Disorder?

Post-disturbing stress disease (PTSD) is a intellectual health circumstance that develops due to trauma. It takes area in humans who've again and again suffered or witnessed a stressful event together with the lack of existence of a cherished one, sexual assault, fundamental twist of fate, herbal catastrophe, domestic violence, and so forth.

Trauma can on occasion be inevitable as we typically commonly tend to stand difficulties at special factors in our life. However, not clearly all people that stories a annoying scenario gets over or moves on from it. People with post-worrying strain sickness regularly exhibit unique traits along with melancholy, immoderate worry, marvel, severe and disturbing thoughts, self-doubt, and having flashbacks of the terrifying occasion which, now and again allows relieve them of the state of affairs.

This intellectual contamination can once in a while be unstable and deadly as it takes a toll on its sufferers primary, to prolonged-lasting damages if now not attended to in time. It little by little begins to affect the way of existence of the traumatized person, how they understand matters and, the human beings round them. PTSD, previously called shell surprise or struggle fatigue syndrome, will have an impact on all males and females regardless of ethnic group, nationality, shade, and tribe. Mental fitness experts frequently believe that put up-annoying strain illness (PTSD) is limited to veterans and the officers of the defense force due to the fact they revel in many traumatizing activities along with terrorist activities, battle, and exclusive fight situations. However, this highbrow fitness condition is not truly restricted to humans of a particular problem or race. It additionally isn't always constrained to a selected age or gender as it takes location in one among a kind age companies (children and adults) and sex. It can seem to absolutely each person, maximum mainly those who've experienced too many unpleasant and life-threatening situations.

It is also vital to word that PTSD differs from Acute stress sickness (ASD) due to the truth signs and signs and signs of ASD make bigger in advance than that of PTSD. ASD can as well be referred to as a precursor to PTSD in some times, definitely no longer all times. While positioned up-disturbing stress sickness varies substantially in phrases of severity, acute pressure contamination symptoms and signs and symptoms and symptoms are commonly slight. ASD can reason PTSD if now not treated on time. Factors which encompass genetics, environment, and data of exposure to trauma can determine why a few people growth PTSD even as others do not, despite the fact that experiencing or after experiencing the same demanding event.

TYPES OF POST TRAUMATIC STRESS DISORDER (PTSD)

Fundamentally, there are 5 (five) kinds of located up-stressful stress sickness (PTSD), all of which work hand-in-hand; and show the price at which the state of affairs progresses inside the patient's mental nation. It is, but, critical as an character to recognize which of the kinds one falls in, having professional a terrifying and tragic state of affairs, to apprehend how precisely to deal with the state of affairs.

The following are the kinds of PTSD.

i.   Normal Stress Response

ii.   Acute Stress Disorder (ASD)

iii.   Uncomplicated PTSD

iv.   Complex PTSD (c-PTSD)

v.   Comorbid PTSD+

i.   Normal Stress Response

It is a normal reaction to strain, a traumatic or demanding occasion that happened these days or within the beyond. Unlike different sorts of PTSD, this sort of response surfaces at the identical time as an person goes via a annoying second. It is regular to answer in a few way to a demanding state of affairs (work or college pressure, injuries, illnesses, injuries, pressure because of a breakup and, so forth). There is not any reason for alarm because it does now not have an extended-time period/bad impact on the person. The satisfactory Treatment for Normal Stress Response is love, care, and manual from the ones residing with the man or woman along Therapy (each man or woman or group).

ii.Acute Stress Disorder

Acute Stress Disorder is regularly misinterpreted as Post-annoying Stress Disorder (PTSD) because of the truth it's miles very similar to PTSD. However, it's miles critical to inform the distinction among ASD and PTSD as they're now not exactly the equal. Acute Stress Disorder (ASD) takes vicinity whilst an person or enterprise organization of human beings is in a life-threatening state of affairs, which has changed their manner of existence. This lifestyles-threatening scenario can be losing a loved one, witnessing a warfare, getting involved in an twist of fate, being in a very abusive dating, being gaslighted, experiencing natural screw ups, and a close to-death revel in. Nevertheless, signs and signs and symptoms of ASD expand inner a month of the disturbing event after which evanesce, in contrast to that of PTSD with extra lingering and chronic signs and symptoms and symptoms. This ASD has an inclination to coexist with distinct highbrow fitness conditions which includes depression and tension and could regularly alternate into PTSD if left untreated. Treatment consists of psychotherapy and Cognitive-behavioral Therapy (CBT)

iii.Uncomplicated PTSD

Uncomplicated PTSD takes region because of one large worrying occasion. It isn't like the alternative types of PTSD due to the fact the individual in this state of affairs has simplest professional wonderful trauma, not more than one disturbing sports. Symptoms of Uncomplicated PTSD encompass having nightmares or flashbacks regarding the event, feeling irritable, having intense mood swings, and a strong preference to overlook approximately and avoid what reminds one of the disturbing activities. Uncomplicated PTSD is rather aware of remedy and remedy as it's far the most diagnosed of all styles of PTSD.

iv.Complex Post Traumatic Stress Disorder (c-PTSD)

Complex Post-traumatic Stress Disorder (c-PTSD), additionally referred to as Complicated Post-disturbing Stress Disorder, happens because of having skilled a couple of traumas over a while (months or years). It could not actually occur once and disappears because it keeps resurfacing. These overly repeated disturbing sports may be the loss of life of a cherished one, domestic violence and emotional abuse, close to-death experiences, publicity to battle, injuries, natural screw ups, and so on. This form of PTSD, mainly, is not with out troubles treatable as it takes longer than ordinary, and the healing fee is prolonged. Unlike unique styles of PTSD, this Complex PTSD calls for brought remedies to ensure proper prognosis and treatment.

v.Comorbid Post Traumatic Stress Disorder

Co-happening problems accompany comorbid Post-disturbing strain ailment. This type of PTSD isn't any distinct from substance use disease and normally comes into lifestyles on the same time as the man or woman has different intellectual health situations. Comorbid Post-disturbing Stress Disorder is a not unusual type because of the truth such some of people be with the aid of one or extra mental fitness conditions.

Some of the co-taking place situations are as follows:

Personality Disorder

Attention Deficit Hyperactivity Disorder (ADHD)

Mood Disorder

Panic Disorder

Anxiety Disorder

Substance Use Disorder

Psychotic Disorder

Depressive Disorder

Bipolar Disorder

Treatment of Comorbid Post-worrying Stress Disorder is alongside the remedy of co-taking place highbrow fitness conditions.

CAUSES OF POST TRAUMATIC STRESS DISORDER (PTSD)

Post-traumatic Stress Disorder (PTSD) generates from a chain of terrifying and annoying events. PTSD can increase from either witnessing or experiencing a traumatic occasion. However, what is taken into consideration worrying varies as all and sundry have one-of-a-kind perceptions approximately situations and activities.

The following are some occasions that could motive Post-demanding Stress Disorder (PTSD)

- Near-demise research

- Loss of a cherished one or doggy

- Accidents (fatal or nonfatal)

- Abuse (both youth, domestic violence, bodily or emotional abuse)

- Sexual Assault or Rape

- Harassment or Bully (racism, sexism, or Body shaming)

- Abduction, Kidnap or being held hostage against self-will

- Experiencing/surviving herbal screw ups at the side of earthquakes, tornados, hate waves, avalanches, storms, volcanic eruptions, floods, hurricanes, and typhoons.

- Witnessing and surviving a Pandemic

•Being convicted for a crime now not committed

•Being diagnosed with a terminal contamination and disorder

•Terrorist assault

•Childbirth headaches (as an example, lack of the kid)

•Being in a line of tough paintings regarding seeing humans that die or are injured often.

•Experiencing a war

•Being tortured

•Daily gas lighting enjoy and others.

Other Risk Factors

•Inherited intellectual health situations consisting of hysteria, Attention deficit hyperactivity illness (ADHD), mood issues, and so on

•Inherited dispositions inclusive of person illness, excessive mood swings, and temperament

•Response of the mind chemical & hormonal adjustments to specific activities or sports activities

•A diploma of the horrible testimonies you've got were given were given had to witness

•Having an hassle with substance misuses along with alcohol or drug dependancy

•Not having loved ones that could characteristic a legitimate manual device

•Getting to appearance a close family member that struggled with nice intellectual fitness situations for years

•Gender additionally performs a critical feature in the improvement of Post-demanding Stress Disorder (PTSD). It is, but, believed that ladies are more likely to be recognized with the intellectual fitness condition than guys

Generally, any terrifying, first-rate traumatic, and lifestyles-threatening occasion that triggers fear, tension, or shock can result in Post-disturbing Stress Disorder.

SYMPTOMS OF POST TRAUMATIC STRESS DISORDER (PTSD)

Post-traumatic Stress Disorder (PTSD), while manifested, can significantly affect the manner of existence of the humans living with it. In some cases, signs and symptoms and signs and symptoms seem a month after the traumatizing enjoy, at the identical time as in others, it seems months or years later. For a few human beings, signs and signs and signs manifestation is quite severe and looks almost immediately, on the same time as signs and symptoms might be mild on the begin and later generate into a few component vital for others. PTSD takes a toll on many those who each had been identified with the illness or not. It affects the college, social, work conditions, and inter-dating with others.

Symptoms fall into 4 (four) lessons, and they may be:

•Intrusion or Re-experiencing Symptoms

•Avoidance/Emotional Numbing Symptoms

•Arousal & Reactivity Symptoms

•Cognition and Mood Symptoms

i.Intrusion or Re-experiencing Symptoms

Symptoms include

A.Having flashbacks of the disturbing event, in addition to feeling the occasion is happening all over again

B.Disturbing and frightening dreams about the worrying event

C.Recurrent mind approximately the event leading to worry

D.The extreme emotional misery that reminds you of the traumatizing event

Intrusive signs and symptoms and symptoms and symptoms have a manner of affecting the regular residing of the man or woman. It also impacts the affected character's thoughts and behavior, thereby changing how the man or woman responds to matters.

ii.   Avoidance/Emotional   Numbing Symptoms

Symptoms embody

A.Steering clean of the places, humans, items, or sports which may be regular reminders of the traumatic event

B.Trying hard now not to recollect the worrying event

C.Occupying the thoughts with certainly one of a kind sports activities sports in order now not to bear in mind the terrifying occasion

D.Feeling indifferent from feelings and emotions

E.Finding it extremely hard in expressing affection in the direction of others

F.Using materials like tablets and alcohol to neglect the traumatizing occasion

iii.Arousal & Reactivity Symptoms

Symptoms consist of

A.Being hyper-vigilant (intense alertness)

B.Difficulty slumbering (insomnia)

C.Being effects startled or anxious (having a fear of the unknown)

D.Guilt-tripping one's self

E.Easily shy, feeling annoying and annoying

F.Feeling irritable and intolerant of others

G.Being aggressive or bursting out angrily

H.Constantly having panic attacks

I.Finding it tough in that specialize in a few detail

iv.Cognition and Mood Symptoms

Symptoms embody

A.Losing interest in matters that changed into fun

B.Having a memory loss as regards the traumatic event that occurred

C.Feeling bad approximately one's self (loss of a immoderate exceptional mind-set concerning your self)

D.Having a loss of take into account in absolutely everybody

E.Feeling insecure

F.Apportioning blame for the occasion. For instance, the loss of existence of a loved one

G.Overwhelming sadness and self-pity.

Physical Symptoms

Physical Symptoms embody

A.Sweating profusely, haziness, migraine, shaking, bad belly scenario, and pains

B.A weakened immune gadget

C.Tiredness and specific pressure-related problems.

Symptoms in Kids

A.Constant Bedwetting

B.Being overly clingy

C.Being now not capable to talk about what is bothering them

D.Having nightmares approximately the annoying occasion

E.Isolating themselves from exclusive humans

F.Having low arrogance

G.Harming themselves in locations that aren't seen

H.Being overly sensitive to matters and troubles

It is genuinely beneficial to appearance out for the ones signs in an character (be it yourself or every person you already know) who has experienced a stressful occasion both currently or inside the past to understand a way to are searching for the assist of highbrow health professionals. The time body with which the event passed off would not rely, as it is in no way too beyond because of are trying to find for assist.

STAGES OF POST TRAUMATIC STRESS DISORDER (PTSD)

There are approximately 5 (five) levels of PTSD which encompass;

1.Impact or Emergency Stage

2.Denial/Numbing Stage

three.Rescue Stage

4.Short term or Intermediate Stage

5.Long time period or Recovery Stage

1.Impact or Emergency Stage

The Impact/Emergency diploma is a diploma that follows the demanding event, in which the affected individual begins offevolved to come back again to terms with the stressful occasion grade by grade and subconsciously. Most times on this Stage, guilt starts to set in alongside self-pity, tension, and receive as real with issues. The person's reaction to the whole lot on this Stage is specifically excessive because the character begins offevolved to avoid humans, misjudge and mistrust human beings because of the fact they revel in anybody is onto/in opposition to them. The period of the effect diploma is predicated upon at the severity of the traumatizing occasion. Symptoms of the effect degree can final for a few hours and occasionally takes days or even months. This Stage specially takes place with those who genuinely survived a war, a near-death revel in, and abuse.

2.Denial/Numbing Stage

It is the Stage wherein the traumatized individual does no longer come to phrases with the occasion. The character starts offevolved to revel in the occasion by no means came about, and his idea is handiest a fraction of his imaginations. Similarly, no longer each traumatized individual receives to revel in the denial stage.

three.Rescue Stage

The rescue stage includes the Intrusive or Repetitive step, wherein the sufferer recognizes that he's traumatized, acknowledges the harm the occasion has brought about and, seeks assist. It may be identified due to the fact the Rescue Stage because the person embarks on the journey to healing.

4.Short time period Recovery or Intermediate Stage

During this Stage, the person with PTSD adjusts again to the every day manner of life he's familiar with in advance than the worrying event. The character on this Stage has gotten to the issue of recuperation as they get love, care, and help from the humans they care approximately and are once in a while upset on the way their cherished ones address them. Healing in all components begins to take region as they encompass who they have got emerge as and sort to be a better version of themselves.

five.Long time period Recovery or Reconstruction Stage

This Stage is also referred to as the Integration Stage. The character gets the vital assist to observe and adapt coping mechanisms to become aware of and go along with the waft on from the trauma. The after-results of PTSD, which encompass tension, nightmares, flashbacks, self-pity, and so on, are treated due to the truth the character learns the manner to govern and beautify on them. The affected character is high-quality to stay everyday life with regular guide from loved ones and mental fitness professionals.

Chapter 2: Complex Post Traumatic Stress Disorder (C-Ptsd)

Complex Post-traumatic Stress Disorder (c-PTSD), furthermore known as Disorder of Extreme Stress Not Otherwise Specified (DESNOS), is the maximum complicated of all Post-stressful Stress Disorder (PTSD) due to its severity and re-prevalence. It effects from a repeated series of annoying activities (together with abuse, loss of life of a cherished one, physical or sexual attack, trafficking, near-loss of life revel in, and the likes), that have been taking place for days, months, or years. This situation is also known as Complicated Post-worrying Stress Disorder.

Symptoms of CPTSD are certainly similar to that of PTSD and unique awesome signs and symptoms and signs and symptoms and signs which are simply associated with it (c-PTSD). According to its name, it's far the most tough to cope with among all of the one in all a type forms of PTSD, and the restoration takes longer. Complex submit-worrying stress illness is much like Borderline Personality illness and Dissociative identification ailment.

Ways wherein Complex Post-disturbing Stress Disorder (c-PTSD) Affects People.

There are several ways in which c-PTSD influences people, and the class is into 7 Domains which incorporates:

• Attachment

• Biology

• Emotional Regulation

• Dissociation

• Behavioral Control

• Thinking

• Self-idea

i.Attachment

The attachment has to do with survivors' trouble developing wholesome barriers, distrusting others, and maintaining aside themselves from humans.

ii.Biology

Biology consists of loss of coordination, elevated scientific situation, and Somatization.

iii.Emotional Regulation

Emotional Regulation involves having hassle expressing one's emotions, mind, and feelings, issue expressing need and dreams.

iv.Dissociation

Dissociation is associated with memory loss and depersonalization (which embody feeling indifferent from frame, thoughts, and emotions).

v.Behavioral Control

Acting out of impulse (being impulsive), being aggressive and irritated, experiencing trouble in following laid down rules and pointers, developing ingesting problems, sleep problems, and substance abuse are all covered in Behavioral Control.

vi.Cognition

Cognition consists of trouble being attentive to a few thing, being absent-minded, having issues with organizing, making plans, studying, lack of ability to perceive matters and making the proper selections.

vii.Self-concept

Self-idea is going by way of manner of the incapability to look self esteem, guilt-tripping oneself over a disturbing event, alongside body shaming.

Problems Associated with Complex Post Traumatic Stress Disorder

The following are the problems related to c-PTSD

•Self-esteem issues

•Emotional Dysfunction

•Relationship Problems

Self-esteem problems: People with c-PTSD often have troubles with vanity. They commonly will be inclined to sense out of vicinity, worthless, and continuously blaming themselves for what befell to them. They won't see a few factor particular coming out of them, and that they write themselves really off in a few instances.

Emotional Dysfunction: They are dysfunctional concerning emotions as they can not inform when they are glad or sad. They get irritated fast, are competitive, out of manipulate, and are commonly beaten with sadness. In precis, they locate it hard to manage and manipulate their feelings.

Relationship Problems: They have issues interacting with wonderful human beings due to a loss of keep in mind in others. Some of them get familiar with the trauma (relying on what delivered about the trauma) and end up entering into relationships with humans that mistreat them simply due to the fact they're trying to find a few closure and validation.

CAUSES OF COMPLEX POST TRAUMATIC STRESS DISORDER (c-PTSD)

Complex Post-annoying stress ailment (c-PTSD) is a repetition of disturbing activities that have an impact on the sufferer in cross returned thru causing lasting adjustments inside the mind. Certain annoying events on the side of sexual attack, abuse (bodily, domestic violence, intellectual, emotional, or little one abuse), trafficking, and kidnap contribute majorly to the improvement of the situation.

The following are the varieties of annoying events that make contributions to the improvement of Complex Post-annoying Stress Disorder (c-PTSD)

A.Continuous abuse (of any kind) and Domestic Violence

B.Childhood forget, abuse, and abandonment

C.Frequently witnessing any of the above

D.Sex trafficking

E.Torture

F.Slavery

G.Genocide

H.Natural failures

I.War

The impact of Complex Post-worrying Stress Disorder (PTSD) on an person is taken into consideration greater grievous if

•The harm evolves due to injuries due to a figure, caregiver, or a relied on person

•Trauma become/is skilled for a completely long time with out help or a way of get away

•The annoying occasion took place at a completely early age and time of the man or woman's lifestyles

• The character experience and handled the aftermath of the event all by means of the use of themselves

•The sufferer remains in touch with the individual accountable for the trauma (in cases wherein a herbal stress would no longer reason the stressful occasion)

SYMPTOMS OF COMPLEX POST-TRAUMATIC STRESS DISORDER

It is essential to recognize Complex Post-worrying Stress Disorder (c-PTSD) emanates from Post-worrying Stress Disorder (PTSD). However, c-PTSD is more advanced regarding the severity and the effect on people who have experienced a extended and ordinary trauma. Symptoms of CPTSD are quite much like that of PTSD however decided thru using greater signs.

The following are the signs and symptoms of c-PTSD

A.Detachment: People with c-PTSD commonly experience indifferent and dissociated from themselves and others. They once in a while experience detached from their frame and mind, that is generally observed via reminiscence loss, making them overlook the traumatic occasion (specially youth trauma).

B.Difficulty Regulating Emotions: They frequently locate it difficult to manipulate their feelings. When unhappy, they do it to the extreme and try to find out a way out of the disappointment, which may also moreover sometimes encompass thinking about suicide and taking drastic measures.

C.A Negative Self-belief: People with c-PTSD can frequently have a tough time seeing themselves in a splendid mild. They may additionally see themselves as now not deserving of love, care, and affection, and at the same time as some factor lousy takes vicinity to them, they may do not forget they deserve it. They are constantly beaten with shame and guilt, feeling answerable for the annoying occasion that occurred. Always wishing they may have accomplished some difficulty to stop the situation.

D.Loss of a machine which means that: This includes losing faith in faith, political gadget, lack of center values and ideals, and feeling overwhelmed with hopelessness

E.Preoccupation with Abuser: The traumatized character receives addicted to locating method to coping with the abuser.

F.Extreme Uneasiness Relating with Others: This consists of the shortage of accept as real with for others because of the trauma gotten from the event. They aren't open to friendships and relationships, typically believing that humans are available to damage you.

G.Relationship Difficulties and problems: People who growth complicated positioned up-traumatic pressure disorder regularly discover it hard to keep a romantic relationship. They will be predisposed not to accept as actual with their companions enough due to the fact they do not even accept as proper with themselves maximum of the time due to all they professional. The scenario thereby makes them domesticate bad relationships each inside the same gender or the opportunity gender.

H.Cognitive Difficulties: This is frequently related to memory loss. In this case, the person forgets what induced the trauma and the manner the occasion completed out, feels indifferent and dissociated from human beings, situations, and topics in standard. The person continuously attempts to alleviate himself from the trauma with the resource of abusing materials which include tablets and alcohol. Seeing a mental health professional or speaking to a trusted pal, colleague, or member of the family can assist with Cognitive issues.

I.Learning Impairment: It is constantly complicated for those nonetheless in school who've superior the situation to pay interest in beauty as they're frequently absent-minded. They normally find it quite hard to pay interest in the school room or assimilate topics as brief as folks who've no longer skilled any annoying or terrifying event.

J.Sleeping & Eating Disorder: People with a c-PTSD state of affairs can regularly find out it difficult to sleep. They are vulnerable to having nightmares or flashbacks concerning the demanding occasion that may have happened lengthy inside the past or is still going on. They additionally lose urge for meals brief and find out meals unappealing, which encompass high pleasant dishes that become as quickly as their high-quality.

K.Painful Loneliness: People with c-PTSD typically revel in by myself even though in a room crowded with humans. They feel disconnected from people in large, coupled with a loss of receive as real with in the human beings round them. They regularly experience lonely and disconnected from their environment, mainly if they may be by myself in a residence.

RISK FACTORS FOR COMPLEX POST TRAUMATIC STRESS DISORDER (c-PTSD)

The Risk elements of Complex Post-stressful Stress Disorder (c-PTSD) may be much like the reasons. Risk elements usually reason a probable boom in the character's chance of developing or redeveloping the illness.

The following are the danger elements for c-PTSD

•Multiple and taking area Traumas

•Trauma from early formative years

•Abuse from a own family pal, member, or relied on person

•History of Abuse of any type: Individuals with a facts of abuse which might be physical, sexual, or emotional, are more likely to growth the complicated put up-stressful disorder often.

•Long-term sexual abuse

•Previous disturbing tales

•Inadequate coping mechanism

•Lack of ethical assist from buddies and family

•Genetic elements and Gender

•Personality developments

•Level of exposure to the annoying occasion

•Living thru worrying and dangerous activities

•Having a facts of other mental health situations or substance abuse

•Dealing with similarly strain after the stressful event, which incorporates losing a interest or domestic, also managing a severe heartbreak, and so on

•Family facts of PTSD, Depression, Anxiety, and special intellectual health conditions

•Being constrained to the walls of a jail cellular can also bring about growing c-PTSD

•Being sincerely hopeless about recovery from the trauma.

Chapter 3: Living With Complex Post Traumatic Stress Disorder (C-Ptsd)

Having to live with c-PTSD may be annoying and draining. Most human beings who've needed to revel in a repeat of fantastic unpleasant occasions, which results in trauma, do now not understand inside the event that they advanced the situation. To stay properly with the state of affairs and manage it, one needs to be knowledgeable approximately what Complex Post-stressful Stress Disorder is and be careful for the signs and signs and signs and symptoms to recognize a way to deal with it. Living with Complex Post Traumatic Stress Disorder can disrupt the way of existence of the character. From having flashbacks, insomnia, and nightmares to having trouble controlling feelings which consist of having angry and being extremely sad. It does now not help every with relationships because it makes the person assemble dangerous relationships. Symptoms with youngsters and adults are quite related however exceptional due to the fact adults cope with conditions in every other manner from kids who find out themselves with the equal hassle. Complex Post-disturbing Stress Disorder (c-PTSD) typically takes a while to deal with because it requires a aware strive from the intellectual fitness professional and that of the patient.

Nevertheless, it is able to be correctly controlled and cared for with a series of Therapy along medication. Joining a beneficial useful resource organization for a start is also very beneficial. One can get higher by using manner of sharing their reviews with like minds (people who completely understand the state of affairs).

Asides from turning into a member of a manual organization, speaking to a depended on person, or seeking out help from intellectual fitness specialists, there are fine sports activities that people with the situation can have interplay in pending the time remedy commences. These sports activities will help boost self-self guarantee and help you stay a nicely-balanced existence.

Activities encompass,

•Exercising often (going for a walk, doing yoga, dancing, taking walks, and the likes)

•Meeting new people

•Activities also include making massive friendships.

•Move to a brand new place (most particularly if the trauma is associated with the modern-day internet website online online)

•Get a modern-day assignment

•Build for your hobby with the resource of studying a book, cooking, writing, or playing an instrument. Whatever your interest is, assemble on it and be committed to it. You can also soak up one if you do no longer have a modern-day hobby. It is generally very therapeutic.

•Practice Mindfulness. Mindfulness generally allows with managing precise troubles alongside complicated post-worrying stress infection, particularly tension, melancholy, and annoying conditions that aren't named. Accept all that you feel after which figure out a way to transport on from the case.

•Keep a magazine; pin down exactly how it's far you feel. You can also use it to keep tabs for your symptoms and signs and symptoms and signs to talk approximately them with someone who can help.

•Get worried on your network thru volunteering if you aren't working. You can get involved peradventure you're running thru using making time to art work with the literacy packages, youths and adults application, medical institution offerings within the community, or even take part in the network sports activities sports.

•Go to Rehab in case you are hooked on alcohol, capsules, cannabis, cigar, and different substances due to the stressful event. Speak for your medical medical doctor approximately your battle with alcohol and unique substances that permits you to refer you to a set or treatment software with the intention to will let you triumph over the war.

BEHAVIORS EXHIBITED

There are powerful behaviors wherein people who boom both PTSD or c-PTSD show off to deal with the state of affairs. These behaviors normally function a coping mechanism for the patients to manipulate and stay via the trauma. However, with the assist of mental fitness specialists, the behaviors exhibited with the aid of patients are modified with nice ones as time is going via. Still, in uncommon instances, the behaviors start to development and in the end get worse over the years. It is higher to look out for those behaviors for your buddies or family members which have experienced repeated annoying sports.

The following are some of the behaviors exhibited via humans with complicated submit-worrying stress disease:

A.Abuse of alcohol and tablets. People who have time and again suffered a sequence of stressful events will be inclined to turn to alcohol, pills, hashish, and cigarettes, for consolation. They get hooked on those substances to put off the pain they're continuously feeling. B.Sex Addiction. People discover themselves hooked on numerous topics on the equal time as traumatized. For a few, it's miles having intercourse with random people to derive moments of pride that feature a prepared distraction for the center problem.

C.Self-damage has end up rampant amongst more youthful people who are traumatized, in particular those tormented by extreme depression. Some people turn out to be lowering themselves with a razor to experience a form of comfort. They relieve themselves of the load of being emotionally careworn via way of inflicting ache on themselves.

D. Inappropriate handling of complaint. Most human beings who've handed via one terrifying occasion or the opposite do now not do nicely with grievance. They burst out angrily at each person that attempts to criticize them.

E. They grow to be humans pleasers. Some become attractive humans virtually because of the truth they may be searching for gratification and validation from those humans and come to be even sadder after they do not get it.

F. They come to be Rebellious. On the opportunity hand, whilst others are attractive human beings, a few are rebellious and do not care approximately their thoughts. This set of people aren't concerned approximately how human beings recognize them. They are aware about their tendencies and are not concerned about how human beings view them.

OTHER RELATED CONDITIONS

1.Borderline Personality Disorder (BPD): Borderline character sickness is a scenario that impacts the manner you spot yourself and perceive others. It affects the manner of lifestyles of the human beings dwelling with it as they transfer moods more frequently than now not, lash out at people for wonderful things that are not nicely well worth getting indignant over. They worry rejection and abandonment and are extensively impulsive, essential to unstable and risky relationships. Like complex submit-traumatic illness, this intellectual health condition known as BPD additionally starts offevolved from early children, but in assessment to c-PSTD, BPD receives higher with time and age and could not commonly upward push up due to multiple traumas.

Symptoms

A.Severe worry of abandonment

B.They are normally having suicidal thoughts/self-damage thoughts because of rejection or worry of being left out and abandoned.

C.Constantly feeling empty on the internal

D.Taking intense measures to avoid being by myself, ignored, deserted, or separated from someone

E.Having a loss of touch with fact, and having intervals of strain-related paranoia

F.Having risky relationships, believing human beings do no longer care, and additionally assuming matters for people

G.They are continuously doing topics out of impulse, being extremely impulsive, and having no regard for the consequences of doing amazing topics which are volatile and terrible to their intellectual us of a and nicely-being. Such behaviors encompass having unprotected intercourse, using recklessly, dabbling into one-of-a-kind pills and alcohol, quitting a method, spending cash on things you do now not want, playing, and so on.

Causes

•Genetics

•Brain Abnormality

2.Disorder of Extreme Stress Not Otherwise Specified (DESNOS): This is much like complex put up-disturbing strain sickness. According to the International Classification of Disease eleventh Edition (ICD-eleven), complex put up-demanding strain illness (c-PTSD) is also called the ailment of excessive stress no longer in any other case focused (DESNOS). Like c-PTSD, DESNOS also takes vicinity due to kids trauma, which incorporates abuse, attack, violence, and struggle. They are every caused via the identical events, and their chance factors and signs and symptoms and signs and symptoms aren't splendid both.

Symptoms

A.Substance Abuse

B.Having trouble in controlling and regulating feelings which incorporates sadness, despair, being annoying, having suicidal mind, and out of manage anger

C.Self-harm and self-mutilation

D.The victim is preoccupied with the mind of the offender and executes plans in seeking out revenge.

E.Being vulnerable to excellent illnesses

F.Feeling ashamed and considering guilt. Supposing you're deserving of the demanding occasion that places your existence in shambles

G.Enduring exchange in person on the aspect of having a distrustful attitude towards others

Causes

•Long time period abuse (baby, physical and sexual)

•Sex trafficking

3.Enduring Personality Changes After Catastrophic Experience (EPCACE): This is displayed via man or woman adjustments after a disturbing event. It is predicated upon at the man or woman's response to the trauma and the manner their existence and attitude in the direction of lifestyles trade after the occasion. The fact is a person's lifestyles can exchange substantially after an encounter with a traumatizing event, and that is what births Enduring Personality Changes after Catastrophic Experience (EPCACE).

Symptoms

A.Anger

B.Aggression

C.A adverse and mistrustful mind-set toward humans and the place at massive

D.Social withdrawal

E.Severe emotions of being on the edge

F.Feeling empty and hopeless

G.Self-injurious and detrimental behaviors

Causes

EPCACE originates from exclusive annoying sports which consist of the death of a cherished one, youngsters trauma together with overlook, abandonment, abuse and attack, domestic violence, natural disasters, conflict, sex trafficking, torture, kidnap and abduction, and other demanding sports.

4.Dissociative Identity Disorder (DID): Dissociative Identity Disorder is characterized thru two or extra separate identities. When someone is said to have DID, the character has a bent to show off notable personalities at outstanding instances. They get to behave in a certainly one of a type way on severa activities and may have unique beliefs at instances. It is a sporadic contamination as an entire lot of humans do no longer show off it. Dissociative identity contamination moreover may be referred to as a couple of or break up character contamination.

Symptoms

A.Anxiety

B.Disorientation

C.Delusions

D.Depression

E.Memory loss

F.Substance abuse which includes tablets and alcohol

G.Suicidal mind and self-damage

Causes

•Physical or sexual abuse at some stage in formative years

•Natural screw ups or one-of-a-type stressful occasions

5.Betrayal Trauma (BT): Betrayal trauma denotes betrayals from relied on human beings on which an man or woman is based upon for survival. Betrayal is portrayed in a specific way, including breaching be given as actual with and violating a person's properly-being and privacy. It is a shape of trauma that still takes place while a trusted company or intimate partner breaks someone's remember resulting in emotional misery and intellectual breakdown. In this case, the betrayed man or woman normally maintains or feels the need to preserve a dating with the betrayer for help and safety, in particular whilst children are involved.

Symptoms

A.Alexithymia: This is a trait identified with the beneficial useful resource of someone's incapacity to provide an reason behind and apprehend the emotions skilled thru oneself.

B. Physical signs and symptoms and symptoms encompass insomnia, a weakened immune gadget, weight troubles, continual fatigue, anger, ingesting, sleeping disease, tremors, shaking uncontrollably, shivering, and gastrointestinal troubles.

C.Anxiety and panic assaults

D.Depression

E.Nightmares

F.Difficulty trusting others

G.Hyper-vigilance

Causes

With Partners

Betrayal trauma is because of emotional or physical abuse, together with infidelities which incorporates digital, emotional, or physical, pornography use, masturbation, precise micro-dishonest behaviors, and particular kinds of violence and manipulation.

With Parents or Caregivers

It consists of Physical abuse together with pointless shouting and spanking. Spanking a toddler for the crimes dedicated by way of the usage of manner of the opportunity siblings can bring about betrayal trauma. When a figure or caregiver is not showing love to a child, attacks a toddler sexually, and fails to shield a infant from harm, the likes can result in betrayal trauma.

COMPLICATIONS

Complex publish-annoying strain sickness (c-PTSD) effects in several complications for the humans residing with it. It disrupts the person's manner of lifestyles and hinders the individual from dwelling a properly-balanced life. Trauma is a terrible condition to have; it adjustments someone's wondering and mindset toward existence.

Complications embody:

•Poor work trendy performance because of unstable intellectual fitness

•Poor college average normal performance

•Unstable friendships and relationships because of the issue in trusting one-of-a-kind people

•Having a low vanity and inferiority complex (in no manner feeling accurate, resulting in the in-recognition of 1's self due to the harm due to the disturbing event)

•Self-mutilation and Being Suicidal

•Alcohol or substance abuse

•Developing other highbrow fitness conditions associated with c-PTSD along with Borderline persona sickness (BPD), a disorder of intense strain now not in any other case centered (DESNOS), amongst one-of-a-kind complications.

REDUCING YOUR RISK

Complex put up-disturbing stress illness (c-PTSD) is an extraordinary and complex scenario. While it could be difficult to avoid specially one is ignorant of their hazard elements. Understanding your characteristic makes it much less complex to navigate. Reducing your risk of developing a highbrow fitness circumstance together with CPTSD and analyzing to stay with it isn't so specific from every distinct. You can only learn how to deal with it as quickly as you have got been diagnosed with having the infection and are seeking for strategies to address it. It is essential to word which you don't blame your self for a few element disturbing activities you have got professional. It is also satisfying to recognize that you are not on my own in the adventure of self-discovery as others are going via the identical scenario or some trouble lots worse. Also, do not be too tough on yourself as there can be no excellent way to address the aftermath of a disturbing crisis. After studying to deal with the highbrow health circumstance, you need to take every step little by little to get a pleasing quit result. Avoid evaluating your situation with some one-of-a-kind's as no mother and father react to topics the same way, even after passing through the same trouble. Everyone handles instances in a unique way, and the readiness and preparedness of humans vary.

Chapter 4: Diagnosis Of Complex Post Traumatic Stress Disorder (C-Ptsd)

Diagnosis of Complex put up-disturbing stress ailment (c-PTSD) is not as smooth as one-of-a-kind highbrow health conditions. The motive being that it's far enormously new and rare. Some scientific docs are not completely privy to what complicated submit-stressful pressure sickness includes. They often misdiagnose sufferers with the c-PTSD situations as they combination-up the signs and symptoms and symptoms and symptoms and symptoms and symptoms and symptoms for one-of-a-kind associated intellectual health situations. Generally, humans are normally right away identified with Post-worrying stress illness (PTSD) specifically due to the reality it's far pretty rampant and suggested amongst fantastic intellectual health issues. However, this is why coming across your signs and signs approximately the manner you revel in can't be over-emphasised. If you watched your analysis is not correct, one manner or another, understanding truly nicely the signs and symptoms you're experiencing is that of Complex Post-traumatic Stress Disorder (c-PTSD). It is really useful to satisfy along with your doctor and supply an reason for the situation of things to them. Complex Post Traumatic Stress Disorder (c-PTSD) is hard to diagnose due to the fact there aren't any specific tests to prove a person has the disorder. Nonetheless, analysis can be accurate, and the situation has severa methods of interrupting one's day by day living.

According to investigate (ICD-eleven), statics has shown that three.Eight% of males and females have Complex positioned up-stressful pressure sickness (c-PTSD) in a check. In evaluation, approximately three.4% of ladies and men were observed to have superior Classic Post-demanding strain sickness (PTSD) out of a complete of 7.2%. To be efficaciously recognized with c-PTSD, it's miles vital not to visit a certified highbrow fitness professional who's properly-versed with such troubles.

Doctors and intellectual health specialists will ask you numerous questions regarding your signs and symptoms and issues after experiencing brilliant worrying occasions. The intellectual fitness professional(s) might need to recognise how frequently you have continued traumatizing occasions. These questions are legitimate and critical in differentiating amongst c-PTSD, PTSD, and precise associated intellectual fitness situations which include BPD, DESNOS, and EPCACE. Emphasis can be made on being very certain and aware about the worrying events which have occurred either these days or inside the beyond so the evaluation can circulate very well.

HELPING SOMEONE LIVING WITH COMPLEX POST TRAUMATIC STRESS DISORDER (c-PTSD)

People with PTSD or c-PTSD typically have a manner of distancing themselves from human beings in elegant, and this is because of the fact they may experience ashamed/stigmatized talking about it, believing that others won't in reality apprehend them. Caring for a person (friend, family, or associate) with a intellectual fitness situation as complicated c-PTSD may be pretty hard but furthermore can be made smooth with a few tips.

TIPS TO HELPING SOMEONE WITH C-PTSD

Provide Them With Support

Providing help for your family who're suffering from complex positioned up-worrying stress sickness may be very critical. The following are the diverse strategies you may show assist to your circle of relatives with the situation

A.Always do not forget their feelings: It is beneficial no longer to take legal hints into your fingers thru suggesting that you recognize what is notable for them due to the truth they may be managing a highbrow health situation. They moreover have feelings, and the emotions are valid, do now not dismiss or invalidate their feelings. Make it vital to are looking for their advise earlier than taking assistive steps.

B.Always learn how to be affected person with them: These subjects take time, and if you truely want to manual them, you need to be affected man or woman with them as recuperation takes pretty a few time.

C.Encourage your family with the complicated PTSD situation to do topics that purpose them to glad consisting of making friends, going out, taking up a interest, exercising, and so forth.

D.Spend enough time with them. Create an on my own time with the patients of a worrying event, spend extremely good time with them, virtually so they understand they will be not on my own in this.

Other subjects you may do consist of;

1.Be a excellent listener; be aware of even the minor matters

People with complicated put up-annoying stress disease may also additionally want to share statistics about the state of affairs/demanding event. When they start speaking approximately the ones things, study no longer to bitch or assume they're nagging. Them speaking approximately it is also a part of the healing method because of the reality now not many people are bold sufficient to speak freely approximately things like that. Talking approximately the manner you feel is also recuperation. You may not commonly do not forget a few element they're saying however, you want to be aware of them regardless.

2.Rebuild their protection and don't forget.

For people who have skilled a traumatizing event, there can frequently be an underlying feeling that the arena is now not steady as they considered it to be earlier than the occasion. In speeding up their recovery, it is crucial to rebuild their consider in themselves and their loved ones. Always make sure they understand they're secure and loose from hazard and harm. Encourage them each day with powerful affirmations; be consistent on the facet of your ensures, presence, and affection. Remind them of their strength and stopping spirit, create workout routines for them through making them select up a interest inside the event that they have none, and continuously remind them of the manner outstanding they'll be and the way grateful you are to have them in your lifestyles.

3.Keep them an extended manner from something (places, human beings, and conditions) as a manner to remind them of the trauma

Keep them a long way from some thing at the way to cause the harm they had been looking to overlook. Avoid the human beings from coming in contact with human beings and places that take them yet again to that vicinity of pain. Help them decide out approaches to answer to flashbacks, panic assaults, and nightmares.

The following are brilliant topics which can cause a traumatized character

•Sounds, factors of hobby, or smells associated with the trauma

•Situations that make them revel in limited to an area (e.G., web site visitors, in a crowded location and hospitals)

•Cemetery, funerals, or getting diagnosed with an disease

•Media Coverage and conversations approximately the trauma

•Negative occurrences

•Anniversaries, dates, unique instances, and events that remind one of the trauma

•People or places that make one recollect the trauma

•Financial inability, Relationships, college, or work

•Old scars they have been given from the annoying occasion or pain

•Feeling helpless, trapped, or out of manipulate

•Having mixed feelings within the direction of a specific hassle and people in preferred, being overly conservative, and feeling resentment inside the course of some thing

four.Help them consist of their Anger and Impulsiveness

By supporting them incorporate their anger and impulsiveness, you are supporting them manipulate their emotions and putting the whole lot in test. Individuals with complicated publish-annoying pressure illness normally have mood swings. At this 2nd, they're happy, and the subsequent, they feel unlucky. This second they may be calm, and the subsequent, they are lashing out. Typically, their emotions are continuously in limbo and a state of quandary. They are constantly exhausted because of the dearth of sleep and can barely control pressure. All the ones are valid symptoms and signs and signs and symptoms to look at out for whilst searching after them, and you may be doing them a outstanding select out by way of the use of finding a way to cope with all of these and containing them.

5.Encouraging them to move for remedy

Caring to your family with c-PTSD will be very important however now not as vital as getting treatment for the situation. The character has to understand the importance of getting dealt with and searching for the help of highbrow health experts, that is the responsibility of the man or woman in price of searching after them (you). Please encourage them to join a help enterprise which is likewise a way of coping with the trauma, communicate to them about the approach of Therapy, and encourage them to move for it.

6.Above all, Take care of yourself

Caring for people with such mental situations can be draining, traumatizing and, hard. You ought to appearance out for yourself in case you want to care for them nicely. You additionally can be traumatized if you do no longer look out for your self. You can also fall into terrible cycles in case you do no longer take preventive measures. Exercise often, get enough sleep, additionally eat healthy and well, and take medicinal tablets even as ill. Lean on relied on friends and own family for guide, communicate to a therapist or counselor approximately the way you enjoy, especially because you started being worried for your beloved with the c-PTSD condition, and find time for your pals, hobbies, and topics you have got have been given an interest in doing. Lastly, take turns with circle of relatives participants (take a wreck at the same time as desired).

PTSD Vs. C-PTSD

Post-demanding strain illness (PTSD) and Complex submit-disturbing Disorder (c-PTSD) are honestly comparable based completely at the reality that they are every advanced while you undergo a disturbing occasion. Therefore, it's miles essential to have a observe their variations as one is greater complex due to extended and repeated disturbing sports.

The differentiations are grouped into 4 (4) subheadings which may be as follows;

•Duration

•Type of Trauma

•Classification

•Statistics

Duration

PTSD

PTSD generally takes place after a unmarried traumatic occasion as it's miles a restricted-time event. Symptoms appear a month after the occasion in maximum instances, at the same time as it takes months or years within the event. Cumulative adulthood trauma is associated specially with PTSD.

CPTSD

CPTSD is related to prolonging and repeated trauma. Symptoms normally take months or years to suffice. They aren't time-constrained, related to co-taking place traumatic studies, which generally start early (formative years). Cumulative teens trauma is strongly related to CPTSD.

Type of Trauma associated

PTSD

PTSD is dependent on excessive injuries, sexual assault, lack of existence of a loved one, herbal disaster, or near-loss of life experience. It is usually reliant on any traumatizing occasion.

CPTSD

CPTSD is commonly relying on formative years abuse, ongoing domestic violence, teenagers neglect about or abandonment, or repeated loss of buddies or own family individuals from an early age. Individuals in this institution are generally but now constantly held captive (bodily or emotionally) via manner of every other character.

Classification

PTSD

PTSD is inclusive in DSM-five (Diagnostic and Statistical Manual of Mental Disorders, fifth Edition) and the ICD-eleven (International Classification of Disease eleventh Revision)

CPTSD

CPTSD is best inclusive within the ICD-11

Statistics

PTSD

•70% of adults have skilled at the least one annoying event

•About 20% of individuals who percentage trauma will develop PTSD

•About eight million humans have PTSD in a given yr

•1 in 13 humans will increase PTSD in some unspecified time in the future of their existence

•three.Four% of men and women were positioned to have evolved PTSD consistent with ICD-11 out of seven.2% of each genders

CPTSD: three.Eight% of women and men have been located to have evolved CPTSD in step with ICD-eleven (International Classification of Disease 11th Edition)

Chapter 5: Prevention Of Complex Post Traumatic Stress Disorder (C-Ptsd)

One can't prevent a annoying event from taking region as we do no longer understand what is going to seem at any given difficulty in our lives. However, after experiencing trauma from a terrifying occasion, feasible save you the trauma from regularly growing into complex put up-traumatic strain illness. These preventive measures, however, need a aware try and intentionally and constantly observe through.

The following are the few steps to reduce the hazard of developing Complex located up-annoying pressure sickness after experiencing any trauma.

1.Talk freely about the occasion with a relied on man or woman

Talking approximately stressful studies allows loads with rushing up the fee of the restoration manner. It is not clean to talk about those objects, but as soon as you could summon the courage to talk approximately it, that limits the trauma's strength over you. And that is the motive why you need to positioned into interest who you need to divulge heart's contents to.

2.Let your self grieve

Grieving is constantly part of the restoration method, specifically after the loss of lifestyles of a loved one. It comes with a curler coaster of feelings which encompass numbness, being unhappy, feeling damage, getting indignant, and with the useful resource of and massive vacancy. It is beneficial you bought the ones feelings whilst they arrive, understand that they are everyday and that these items take time to heal. Do now not be too difficult on yourself at the same time as the emotions set in, include them, and discover ways to glide on from them.

3.Work to place an give up to traumatic thoughts

It is indeed normal to have disturbing mind after witnessing or experiencing a traumatizing event, along side announcing sure such things as you are not accurate enough, you may die, you aren't going to make it. And often, the ones thoughts motive worry, anxiety, despair, and the likes, this is why it's far critical to apprehend those terrible thoughts and replace them with wonderful ones.

4.Learn to understand triggers

It is also critical to understand subjects that reason the trauma and avoid or discover ways to stay with them. It can be remarkable sounds, human beings, a selected fragrance, a place, or occasions that remind you of the trauma.

5.Disconnect yourself from the motive

Disconnecting the triggers will help lessen your threat of developing Complex submit-traumatic strain disease. You get to detach your self from the triggers through the use of manner of operating through the feelings that can help you disconnect from them.

6.Seek Therapy

Seeking Therapy and the help of highbrow fitness specialists in the course of or after trauma will help you from developing c-PTSD due to the reality they may be professional and experienced folks that can offer you with all the critical assist and information you want in getting over the trauma.

TREATMENT OF COMPLEX POST-TRAUMATIC STRESS DISORDER

Complex put up-annoying strain disease (c-PTSD) is constantly a brand new and rare situation that makes it a chunk complex to deal with. Mental health experts are though working on severa treatment alternatives. However, CPTSD can be dealt with with the equal treatment plans as PTSD. These remedies can reduce symptoms and symptoms and symptoms and assist you manage the scenario well.

Treatments for Adults embody:

1.Psychotherapy

2.Eye Movement Desensitization And Reprocessing Therapy (EMDR)

3.Exposure Therapy

four.Cognitive Behavioral Therapy (CBT)

Psychotherapy

Psychotherapy is also known as speak therapy. It is a psychological remedy that consists of talking with the therapist or intellectual fitness expert approximately your bad notion patterns, both on my own or in a set. It consists of the use of unique strategies to enhance the mental properly-being of a person or institution of people.

Eye Movement Desensitization and Reprocessing Therapy (EMDR)

EMDR enables humans with PTSD and c-PTSD through a method in which the therapist triggers their reminiscence via the usage of making them hold in thoughts the disturbing occasion and desensitize the traumatic mind and recollections. This technique lets in the person don't forget disturbing recollections at the same time as no longer having an adverse response to them.

Unlike fantastic remedies that reputation in particular on changing the disturbing recollections, this EMDR makes a speciality of converting the way the reminiscence stores within the mind, thereby limiting the difficult symptoms and effects it has at the individual.

Exposure Therapy

This remedy helps sufferers with PTSD and c-PTSD face and triumph over their fears. This Therapy which is likewise powerful for treating anxiety sickness commonly breaks the sample of worry and avoidance by way of the usage of growing a solid environment, making the affected person receives higher, and in the end triumph over some issue is threatening them psychologically.

Cognitive Behavioral Therapy

Initially designed for treating most effective melancholy, this treatment has helped treat distinct intellectual health situations which encompass PTSD, CPTSD, Borderline man or woman ailment (BPD), tension sickness, obsessive-compulsive sickness (OCD), and psychotic problems. Like psychotherapy, CBT is also a speakme remedy that facilitates individuals with intellectual health conditions control their signs and symptoms and signs and symptoms and signs with the useful aid of converting how they recognize matters and behave. It targets to help the patient cope with troubles which may be pretty overbearing in a extra top notch manner.

Tips on a way to govern and treat children with c-PTSD include:

Complex publish-traumatic stress sickness develops in kids not noted, maltreated, or abused with the useful resource of mother and father or caregivers.

1.The first step is identifying and addressing the threats to the kid's safety and intellectual stability

2.The advantage of the child and caregiver need to be maximized and retained

three. The remedy plan and analysis need to be affordable and help to boost the kid and caregiver

four.With whom, how, and at the same time as the disturbing reminiscences are addressed need to be decided

five.Psychosocial crises need to be avoided and managed well

MEDICATION FOR COMPLEX POST TRAUMATIC STRESS DISORDER (c-PTSD)

There are not any precise medicinal drugs for treating c-PTSD. However, some drug remedies used for treating despair also can reduce signs and symptoms of complicated put up-traumatic pressure disease (c-PTSD). These medicinal drugs are greater effective even as blended with psychotherapy. They may be each taken inside the brief or long time which is purely relying on the severity of symptoms and signs and symptoms and effectiveness of Therapy.

Antidepressants and anti-tension applied in treating complicated located up-worrying strain contamination ought to excellent be prescribed and administered thru a professional and ought to never be self-prescribed.

RECOVERY AND OUTLOOK

Recovery from complex placed up-worrying strain illness generally takes time and calls for a aware and planned try and boost up the rate. The scenario has a bent to disrupt the way of life of a few humans for a extra extended length, on the same time as for others, it is for a shorter period. Nonetheless, with a bargain commitment to Therapy and drugs, you can recover and get your existence another time from complex PTSD.

There are three tiers of complicated post-stressful pressure sickness (c-PTSD) healing.

These ranges sum up all you can do to rush up the restoration fee, and they will be as follows

1.Establish Safety and Stabilization in c-PTSD healing

Having advanced complicated PTSD, the concept of being dangerous and destabilized begins to rule the thoughts. The individual feels plenty much less solid while they may be round human beings and particular locations. Their worried gadget is tousled, thereby getting deregulated, and , you get panic attacks from nowhere. Once you could set up your protection and balance thru the help of Therapy and medicines, you begin to flow into freely while no longer having to fear. You start feeling consistent and begin to guide your self while not having to rely upon a person else actually.

2.Practice Remembrance and Embrace the Mourning Period

Avoidance is one of the signs and symptoms of complex PTSD, which continues recollections of the disturbing revel in away and makes it unresolved. To definitely get over the condition, you want to virtually be given those thoughts and recollections of the occasion on the same time because it comes. You have a tendency no longer to transport earlier via the usage of not thinking about what has passed off in the beyond. If the stressful event concerned the dying of a loved one, it is very plenty advisable to mourn the person and all of the things you have got lost because of the trauma, so your thoughts can be free from the thoughts of being caged. EMDR, CBT, and Psychotherapy are usually very beneficial at some stage in this Stage.

three.Reconnecting With Society

Reconnecting with society is the last Stage of the restoration technique. In this Stage, the character accepts all that has took place as a part of the unavoidable schooling in existence. They intend to move on from the trauma via reconnecting with society, family, and buddies. They end up greater active in the affairs in their lives, their network, and that during their cherished ones. They empower themselves, beautify their abilities, take price in their lives, and revel in in ordinary manage of their beyond, gift, and destiny.

Chapter 6: What Is Trauma?

The word 'trauma' may be traced lower returned to the Greek language. It is immediately translated to mean wound. In the medical region, Trauma is known as a bodily wound. In social sciences and well-known way of life, Trauma is used to give an explanation for nice evaluations inside the global.

Trauma is an excessive mental reaction that takes location while an man or woman is faced with a totally worrying situation. It is a enormously emotional response or response to a distressful, disruptive, and overwhelming experience. When such situations arise, it's far not unusual for the immediate reaction to be marvel and denial. These reactions are brief-time period or instant reactions as they may very lastdays to each week. There also are extended-term effects of Trauma on an character.

Trauma is a subjective occasion. The degree to which one individual is suffering from such destabilizing lifestyles sports is dependent on the man or woman. There are situations whereinhumans experience the identical shape of disturbing occasion however have very unique responses to it. One character might also need to have a worrying response, and the other may not. One out of 4 adults tales post-disturbing stress after a annoying occasion. One out ofchildren who revel in a stressful occasion develops a disturbing strain response. Trauma motives a massive shape of intellectual and emotional reactions. The symptoms that comply with may be brief-term or lengthy-time period. When the severity of signs and signs and symptoms persists and will boom over time, that is categorized as an extended-term response, and an illustration of the development of a intellectual ailment called Post-annoying Stress Disorder. This has a protracted-time period effect on an person's well-being.

Trauma exists in a continuum. In latest instances, the word trauma has emerge as increasingly famous in our way of lifestyles.

The phrase modified into to start with connected to or particular to navy veterans, and the facts of the PTSD analysis can be traced over again to them. It modified into not till the 1980's that PTSD modified into diagnosed as a analysis. Since then, the recognition of Trauma and its pervasive influences on our society is now notably unfold and identified. There are nice events that humans can without problems component out as demanding. However, special occasions can not be with out troubles classified as traumatic. These occasions and critiques can motive worrying stress and significantly impact human beings at some point of their lives, however they every so often flow left out or unidentified as traumatic.

An instance of this will be a prolonged and normal bullying enjoy inside the direction of youth. This event won't be diagnosed as worrying until its outcomes are carefully studied. There is an big impact at the individual's revel in of self, bear in mind, perceptions of relationships, ideals approximately the area, reactivity, worried gadget, avoidance, and dissociation.

Trauma consists of abuse, forget about, abandonment, and greater complex demanding forms of loss. Unfortunately, there can be a failure to apprehend how dangerous neglect approximately and abandonment may be. It is less smooth to become aware of as acute, active Trauma, or a traumatic event. Neglect and abandonment are the absence of care and the dearth of getting emotional, social, and physical needs met. Sometimes, the annoying results of forget about approximately and abandonment are extra hard to heal from than the outcomes of active Trauma.

Several conditions may be categorized as disturbing, along with conflict, rape, molestation, injuries, herbal failures, and losing a loved one. Traumatic events cause Trauma, and people sports activities might be isolated. This way the occasion might have been a one-off, and there may be little to no possibility of getting a repeat. It can be one occasion that befell inside the beyond or a fairly cutting-edge gift. Traumatic occasions can also be repeated or ongoing activities.

Trauma may be evolved through witnessing a demanding experience taking place to someone else. This is called vicarious or 2d-hand Trauma.

Research suggests that about 70 percent of adults within the United States of America have skilled a few stressful event at the least as quickly as. That is about 223.Four million people. Roughly 33 percentage of youngsters who've been exposed to violence will increase Trauma on the manner to bring about Post-demanding strain disorder. It is also critical to phrase that 1.Forty five billion people skilled battle amongst 1989 and 2015. An predicted 354 million person struggle survivors have PTSD.

According to the global form of ailment via the arena health enterprise and the diagnostic and statistical guide for intellectual troubles, a stressful occasion is one wherein there may be publicity to loss of life or threatened demise. There is also exposure to real or threatened or extreme harm or real or threatened sexual violence. Traumatic sports activities are characterized thru using an excessive enjoy of powerlessness and excessive disruption of ideals and expectancies. In maximum times, the man or woman has no control over the situation and has turn out to be a sufferer of the condition or one-of-a-type human beings. A demanding experience is a helplessness that takes place through inner or outside elements. In addition, traumatic conditions have a propensity to shatter fundamental assumptions about self and others. It creates self-doubt and a drastic reduction interior the texture of self-worth. It creates a vulnerability that did not exist in advance than. The idea that the area is a benevolent area, and the consider in others is destroyed.

Being exposed to Trauma isn't an terrific incidence, and absolutely everyone can be tormented by Trauma, which includes youngsters and teens. A global mental survey of adults turned into carried out among 70,000 people from 24 countries. The records derived from this survey observed out that ultimately in their lives, the bulk of participants skilled Trauma. 70.Four percentage of the members expert at least one form of traumatic event. 14 percent had professional intimate accomplice violence (IPV) or sexual violence. 34.Three percent had professional immoderate injuries or accidents. 22.Nine percentage had professional physical violence. Thirteen.1 percentage had professional war-associated Trauma. 34.1 percentage had expert the unexpected or violent death of a loved one, and 35.7 percent experienced Trauma from witnessing a traumatic occasion that took place to someone else; this grow to be typically the lack of existence or existence-threatening contamination of a loved one. These findings display that it's far common to be uncovered to and experience seriously scary conditions to your lifetime.

TYPES OF TRAUMA

Experiencing trauma isn't uncommon. A huge sort of human beings in their person existence have professional some form of Trauma, whether it's miles life-changing, disruptive, or not. This Trauma remains with us for good-bye that it becomes unhealed or unresolved Trauma. The types of Trauma are labeled in step with the frequency of worrying sports that an character research. There are three maximum essential kinds of Trauma inclusive of:

•Acute Trauma: This is Trauma that comes from a single traumatic and dangerous event. This Trauma may be classified as a small t or massive T trauma, depending on the character and the area. These activities is probably injuries, rape, assault, or a natural disaster. These sports activities are typically intense to threaten an character's emotional and physical safety. Such events additionally create an prolonged-lasting have an effect on on an character's mind and, if not professionally dealt with, can have an impact at the manner the person thinks and behaves. Symptoms that imply that an individual is stricken by acute Trauma encompass excessive anxiety, confusion, loss of capability to have restful sleep, feeling disconnected from their surroundings, whole lack of self-care, infection, and aggressive conduct. House fires, automobile accidents, witnessing an act or acts of violence, herbal disasters, and assault are also examples of activities that would cause acute Trauma.

•Chronic Trauma: As in opposition to acute Trauma because of a completely particular traumatic event, this type of Trauma develops at the same time as an individual is exposed to a couple of lengthy-term, repeated, and prolonged distressing worrying activities over an prolonged duration. Such events encompass warfare, bullying, ongoing abuse, home violence, and clinical Trauma. It is critical to have a look at that it degenerates into continual Trauma on the identical time as left untreated. Symptoms of chronic Trauma do not seem without delay. These signs may want to ground years after the event has occurred. The symptoms and signs and symptoms and symptoms that propose the presence of continual Trauma are frequently miserable and may seem inside the form of emotional outbursts, tension, excessive anger, flashbacks, fatigue, and exhaustion. Physical signs and symptoms that accompany this shape of Trauma encompass nausea, body pain, and headaches. People who be bothered through persistent Trauma will be predisposed to have immoderate take delivery of as true with issues, which have an impact on their private and professional relationships. Professional help is required to ensure they get higher efficaciously and in top time from such signs and symptoms and signs and symptoms.

•Complex Trauma: This type of Trauma develops due to publicity to more than one and sundry annoying reviews or sports.

Individuals with complicated Trauma had been exposed to severa trauma-inducing activities. In maximum times, people with complex Trauma grew up in abusive, chaotic, and neglectful homes. They then experience distinct varieties of Trauma, that might fall underneath the extreme or continual trauma training. These activities are generally within the context of interpersonal relationships. These annoying sports might also moreover moreover occur inner a particular time frame. It may additionally deliver the character the sensation of being trapped inside the state of affairs. Complex Trauma has a profound and extreme effect on the thoughts of the people that enjoy it. It influences an character's primary health, relationships, concept styles, behaviors, and performance at paintings or faculty. It is not one-of-a-kind to but isn't always uncommon in humans who have been patients of youth abuse, forget about approximately, home violence, circle of relatives disputes, kidnapping, trafficking, and first rate repetitive occasions like civil unrest.

There are different types and lessons of Trauma, at the side of:

•Big T trauma: This form of Trauma is a single incident occasion that has excessive and lasting influences on the person who has professional it. The signs and symptoms of this form of Trauma are likened to position up-annoying strain ailment. Individuals that be tormented by approach of big T trauma be troubled by way of bad feelings, intrusive mind, flashbacks, and nightmares. This ought to result from activities like acts of terrorism, battle, sexual attack, and extended periods of sexual and emotional abuse.

•Small t trauma: This type of Trauma stems from non-public occurrences or events. Examples of small t trauma sports activities encompass divorce, normal academic, art work-associated, and monetary stress, and the dearth of a project, to mention some. All different disturbing activities that are not included below the massive T trauma fall beneath this elegance. Small t trauma, no matter its call, does now not reduce its capability to seriously disrupt your lifestyles if it's miles left unchecked and unprocessed.

•Relational Trauma: This is Trauma in the context or confines of a courting. It is the after-impact of overlook approximately, abuse, abandonment, and betrayal. People who be affected by approach of relational Trauma have generally been betrayed via people they cherished, trusted, and relied on implicitly. These people, in maximum times, face mental and behavioral demanding situations. They moreover find it hard to construct interpersonal relationships and deal with a number of existence's annoying conditions. This shape of Trauma additionally distorts an individual's self-picture. There is youth and character relational trauma.

•Collective Trauma: This is Trauma that occurs whilst a whole enterprise of people has a worrying revel in based totally on their group identity. It need to affect the entire society or a small group like the circle of relatives, race, or nationality. Traumatic activities that might cause collective trauma embody famine, struggle, herbal disasters, aircraft crashes, famine, drought, or pandemics like the COVID 19. Other examples of collective Trauma in facts are the Atomic bombing of Hiroshima and Nagasaki, American slavery, the holocaust, and the 9-11, 2001, terrorist assault. It is essential to word that those sports do not need to be skilled in my opinion to make an effect. Just searching the records being relayed can be disturbing.

•Racial Trauma: It is also known as race-primarily based worrying strain. This is Trauma that takes area because of emotional and intellectual injuries resulting from encounters with racial bias and exposure to racial abuse inside the media. This Trauma impacts nearly each hassle of an man or woman's lifestyles, specifically their ability to have relationships, cope with art work or school, and generally enjoy steady. Racial discrimination is the primary risk element for racial Trauma. This form of Trauma isn't always unusual amongst marginalized races, and similarly they revel in higher expenses of publish-worrying strain sickness.

•Financial Trauma: This shape of Trauma takes area due to inadequate fee variety to cope with goals as they upward thrust up or an surprising economic loss, foreclosures with the resource of the financial agency, or dropping a large amount of money to fraud. It is also because of the stress of having inadequate fee variety to care for self and own family. Financial Trauma takes place whilst a person's earnings is insufficient to satisfy their charges. Losing a undertaking or the primary supply of profits can reason this. In most times, the impact of this Trauma is so excessive that it disrupts an person's art work-lifestyles balance and reasons destabilizing emotional and physical distress. Financial Trauma impacts human beings on a bodily, emotional, and cognitive degree. Physical signs and symptoms like insomnia, concerned electricity, jittering, and hyper-reactivity to situations remind them of the modern-day economic loss. In some instances, the telephone ringing can cause cause, specifically while the character has awful debt or debt creditors are continuously soliciting for their cash. Emotional symptoms and symptoms embody difficulty exciting and playing their preferred interests, incapacity to be intimate with cherished ones, sadness, and despair. Some cognitive signs encompass horrible mind and ideals about self and their environment.

•Ancestral Trauma: It is also referred to as inherited Trauma. There is lots of studies to recognize and verify how Trauma faced through ancestors can also moreover have an impact at the triumphing and future generations. Several studies have positioned that kids of the holocaust survivors (an instance of collective Trauma) are hyper-vigilant and are at risk of fear. Research findings show comparable tendencies in the youngsters of Vietnam War veterans. These

98

inclinations may also moreover persist into adulthood.

It is important to observe that the experience of a trauma you have is placed inner your way of life, notion system, and perceptions of the arena, the manner you are making enjoy of factors spherical you. The manner you've got interaction with society and method your testimonies is related to and heavily embedded for your cultural, racial, and non secular historical past. This is a exceptional motive whyhuman beings may enjoy the same occasion, and one among them may additionally moreover see and respond to it as a stressful event, and the opportunity might not.

A lot of humans do no longer like to talk about Trauma. Although it's far a difficult undertaking and is probably painful, speaking approximately it aids the restoration and recuperation approach in a few times. Neuroscience studies suggests that after an person is requested to keep in thoughts a disturbing revel in, the left hemisphere of the thoughts, which controls the method of rational perception, choice making, language, and speech, is going offline. In evaluation, the right hemisphere of the mind becomes overactive. When an character is requested to maintain in thoughts a annoying enjoy, their Broca's region that has to do with speech and language will become barely useful. There is a whole lot less hobby on this thoughts place, which permits that it's miles difficult to talk approximately Trauma. Sometimes there are not any phrases to give an explanation for or describe the emotions and thoughts about the revel in.

While a few people find it tough to talk approximately it, others have had distressing reports however do now not label them as Trauma. Some don't have any recollection of the worrying reviews in their lives. It is not uncommon for annoying research to be suppressed; they haven't any conscious memory of the occasion. This is a common state of affairs, especially at the same time as the disturbing scenario happens in the first few years of existence. The hippocampus, the part of the brain that holds memories and mind, does now not completely expand untilor three years vintage. Someone who skilled Trauma before they wereought to in all likelihood now not have any reminiscence of it. The strain hormone cortisol can effect the hippocampus' capability to keep recollections while you are overly pressured. This consists of whilst you are experiencing overwhelming worrying stress. It is likewise common to have instances in which an man or woman remembers handiest bits and quantities of the occasion however no longer the complete occasion. It isn't always uncommon for traumatic recollections to be fragmented, incoherent, and fuzzy.

Traumatic recollections additionally normally generally have a tendency to floor at extraordinary elements of an character's existence. They might not keep in mind a demanding enjoy proper now, however they will floor in a while, mainly when they experience greater consistent in their lives and relationships.

CAUSES OF TRAUMA

Adverse sports that cause Trauma generally have a tendency to impact the individual's intellectual fitness and emotional stability. Some trauma is prompted bodily due to intense bodily injuries which have an impact at the frame by myself. This is called medical Trauma. On the alternative hand, intellectual Trauma impacts an person's intellectual and bodily health and effects in pretty some the symptoms already said above. Trauma is due to experiencing worrying events like

•Bullying

•Childbirth

•Death of a cherished one

•Loss of a assignment

•Accidents

•Kidnapping

•Wars and civil unrest

•Rape and molestation

•Assault; all styles of attack

•Neglect and infant abuse

•Domestic violence

•Severe contamination and damage; the analysis of a terminal contamination is enough to motive Trauma.

Although Trauma is attributable to experiencing worrying occasions, it isn't always constantly related. People may also have Trauma from simply witnessing a mainly gruesome occasion taking place from a distance. Children and young adults are most susceptible to this condition, even though safety operatives and fitness care professionals are also inclined. These people want to be evaluated psychologically after witnessing a traumatic event to make certain the emotional nicely-being of all people worried.

SYMPTOMS OF TRAUMA

The signs that appear because of trauma range from moderate to immoderate, and on the identical time as there are numerous reasons and a widespread range of symptoms and signs and symptoms, there are a few clean signs and symptoms to look out for. People who have experienced demanding activities have a tendency to be in denial, disoriented, and shaken. They normally generally tend to withdraw in social settings; they do no longer respond nicely to conversations and do now not act how they usually would. One of the most commonplace signs and symptoms and signs of Trauma is excessive anxiety. It can appear in edginess, temper swings, bad interest, irritability, restlessness, and not unusual nightmares. These symptoms and signs are not unusual but inexhaustible. Every individual responds to Trauma in a distinct manner. Sometimes the symptoms can flow neglected through the people and their cherished ones. Several factors determine how a disturbing occasion will affect an individual, along side:

•The characteristics and behavioral kinds of the man or woman

•The presence or absence of various intellectual fitness problems

•Previous publicity to annoying occasions

•The kind and characteristics of the demanding occasion

•The person's records and technique to managing emotions

Trauma signs may be divided into :

•Emotional and intellectual signs and symptoms and signs: Trauma manifests itself via emotions. It triggers plenty of negative feelings. A few emotional symptoms and symptoms embody denial, anger, guilt, disgrace, worry, unhappiness, confusion, helplessness, tension, and excessive, uncontrollable emotional outbursts. Victims of Trauma will be predisposed to redirect their emotions or lash out at their cherished ones. Most time, they push their cherished ones away. This is a large purpose why buddies and households of trauma patients locate it hard to manipulate. It is critical to understand and understand emotional signs and symptoms and symptoms and signs that seem after a stressful event. This makes the restoration approach less difficult for the victim and their loved ones. Flashbacks, intrusive mind, and nightmares also are highbrow signs and symptoms and signs and symptoms. These symptoms are very distressing as they make the victim replay and relive the occasion of their minds.

•Physical signs and symptoms: Trauma additionally causes bodily symptoms and symptoms. The physical symptoms and signs can be as debilitating and alarming because the pain of an contamination or bodily damage. Some of the most not unusual physical symptoms and symptoms encompass lethargy, panic assaults, fatigue, headaches, frame pain, hassle respiration, expanded coronary coronary coronary heart rate, sweating, and digestive or stomach problems. The inability to cope with superb situations reminds them of the annoying occasion. In a few instances, the man or woman might also moreover additionally experience hyperarousal. This is a scenario wherein trauma sufferers are in a ordinary u . S . A . Of alertness. This situation makes it hard for them to sleep, resulting in fatigue, restlessness, and insomnia.

•Apart from tension and melancholy, substance abuse can give up end result from Trauma.

EFFECTS OF TRAUMA

When you witness some element very annoying, scary, and distressing, the results of this occasion linger prolonged after the real danger is over. Its consequences can be felt for your emotions, frame, and thoughts. Also, it can be each brief or lengthy-time period. The prolonged-time period effects of Trauma are immoderate and really excessive. These consequences can remaining for some weeks or years. The effects of Trauma ought to be addressed as fast as possible to keep away from the scenario becoming everlasting. The quicker the signs and symptoms and signs and results are recognized and controlled, the quicker the recuperation. The prolonged-term outcomes of Trauma are so extreme that it tampers the survivors' pleasant of existence and influences their interpersonal relationships. The most effective difference among Trauma's quick and lengthy-time period outcomes is their severity. Short-time period results are visible within the steady temper swings, denial, and shock exhibited proper now after the enjoy. If those temper swings very last longer than a month, the prolonged-term results are in play. Some of the intense consequences of Trauma include:

•The urge to self-damage and suicidal ideation: People adapt self-unfavorable behaviors like lowering to control. In some times, they emerge as suicidal. Their mind are focused on locating strategies to give up their lives.

•Anxiety and severe depressive episodes: A lot of humans that go through disturbing sports have a propensity to increase a mistrust of every person and the entirety, specifically in the event that they were patients of rape, attack, molestation, or bullying. They normally tend to keep their shield up and are continuously alert. They worry plenty and are susceptible to concerned breakdowns. They can with out problems turn out to be paranoid. In a few conditions, they end up withdrawn and lose interest in things that previously delighted them. They will be predisposed to be sad and depressed most of the time.

•Emotional dysregulation: Several individuals who have confronted disturbing conditions will be predisposed to have little or no control over their feelings and the way they react to high-quality conditions. They will be predisposed to be very prickly and overly competitive about the littlest topics. They have masses of indignant outbursts.

•Alcohol and substance abuse: This is every other one of the an awful lot less healthful techniques human beings cope with their Trauma. It is horrible as it results in dependancy, some other mental fitness trouble. Unfortunately, alcohol and drug abuse are common among human beings handling Trauma. Research shows that many people handling Trauma cave in the rabbit hole of dependancy.

•Inability to maintain relationships: Due to the emotional outbursts, anxiety assaults, depressive episodes, and social withdrawal, they generally tend to push people away by using twist of destiny. This frequently reasons a pressure on the relationship and frustration gadgets in. In some situations, the trauma patients are seen as uncooperative and tiresome.

•The improvement of PTSD: This is a likely effect of Trauma. The development of PTSD is sort of inevitable even as the signs and symptoms and symptoms and symptoms of Trauma do now not decrease of their severity or final longer than they need to.

THE 4-F TRAUMA RESPONSES

It is essential to examine the human mind and mind are designed to defend you from risk. When you're in danger, the thoughts works in a exceptional manner to make certain that you are nicely included from the chance. If an man or woman lives in a war-torn quarter or an environment in which they witness horrible events, the thoughts turns into defensive. This prompts the thoughts and body to answer simply so the opportunities of survival are extensively stronger. The thoughts activates a protection response in which unique quantities of statistics about the occasion are saved in recollections. This permits the mind right away spot those unique symptoms and symptoms of danger in the destiny. They function an early warning device primarily based on past reports.

The thoughts has some protection responses which will automatically motive to guard you in a volatile scenario. They are called trauma responses. It is that out of control knee-jerk response in a stressful scenario. The pre-frontal cortex is the a part of the mind that controls thinking, reasoning, and judgment. That a part of the thoughts is going clean even as brought approximately or has a trauma response, similar to Broca's location that controls speech. The thoughts does all it is able to to preserve you safe, as a end result those computerized responses. There are four one among a kind types of trauma responses, collectively with;

•Flight: This is an strength surge inside the frame that permits get you and your family far from risk speedy, mainly on the same time because it isn't a situation you may address or the chance appears not possible to surmount. Tense muscle tissue, sweating, shaking, and the need to apply the relaxation room are symptoms. There are also distinctive physical adjustments, and those changes assist with the power to guard ourselves. The flight response can be wholesome or bad. A healthy flight response will will let you depart toxic and abusive relationships and conversations. It will let you nicely check probably unstable conditions and put off your self from them. It is critical to have a healthy flight reaction that will help you be alert sufficient to revel in actual hazard. People who be stricken with the aid of unresolved Trauma have a tendency to perceive the whole lot as a hazard. An dangerous flight trauma reaction consequences in panic, constant fear, obsessive and now and again compulsive inclinations, an inability to be but and busy, or inclinations to be a workaholic.

•Fight: This is the trauma reaction in which the mind is prompted to position up an severe fight towards anything or man or woman that proves to be potentially unstable. When the fight response kicks in, you grow to be shielding and irritable. It is referred to as a self-preservation reaction. It may also be protective your self in a state of affairs where someone is being abusive, disrespectful, or demeaning. Fending off an animal that threatens you is an appropriate combat response. This combat response will can help you learn how to be assertive, establish wished limitations, and shield your self and your family even as crucial. Although, in instances in which an man or woman has been uncovered to prolonged Trauma, the fight reaction can be awful and unfavourable to their fitness. It can also purpose bullying, disorderly behavior, feelings of entitlement, narcissistic tendencies, and controlling behaviors. It is not uncommon for folks who engage of their combat response to be on excessive alert and ready to combat constantly.

•Freeze: The freeze reaction is an entire lot less well-known than the fight and flight responses. It is a trauma reaction that reasons you to pause in preference to on foot away or stopping. It is triggered in a situation in which you can't run away, get unfastened, or win a combat. It also may be known as dissociative.

The mind pumps the body with a hormone that acts as a ache reliever; it moreover physically and emotionally disconnects you from what goes on so you do no longer experience the general brunt. This prevents you from experiencing the horrors that accompany that scenario. This response is commonplace in instances in that you're trapped and no longer capable of escape, overpowered thru the perpetrator, or physically and sexually harmed. The freeze trauma reaction additionally can be healthy or awful. The healthful freeze response lets you be extra conscious, aware, or within the present second. It is to be had in on hand while you want to have a have a look at a situation objectively. This response will become awful even as there is unresolved Trauma concerned. Children with abusive mother and father or caregivers will be inclined to be unnaturally quiet and even though as feasible to avoid triggering their discern's wrath. Some people come to be so crushed by fear that they can't flow into. When risky, it could motive isolation and dissociation, hassle in making choices, taking movement, fear of attempting out new matters, brain fog, and regular zoning out. •Fawn: This reaction is normally called people-right. It is a state of affairs wherein you try and appease the factor or humans that purpose stress and the feel of being threatened. This trauma reaction isn't always unusual in people raised in narcissistic family dynamics. This is a state of affairs where your primary caregiver, a person speculated to maintain you safe, is the identical character inflicting damage. Children are resilient as they short examine techniques to cope with their situations however have a propensity to have a observe maladaptive coping competencies or mechanisms. Children in this case look at they're not steady but though crave the protection and protection the figure is supposed to provide. This has a tendency to reason a dissociative break up as the kid is stuck between looking to run away and in spite of the truth that craving the love and care of the decide. Since each conditions aren't possible, the fawning trauma response is birthed. This is a state of affairs wherein the kid has to pacify, please, and appease the caregiver in any manner viable to attempt to avoid extra abuse. This seems like an fantastic sufficient coping mechanism but becomes unhealthy over time. Children who've to stifle their dreams and emotions to assuage, please, and soothe others, will be predisposed to develop into adults who are dissociated from themselves. They experience a lack of self. Many of them emerge as numb and disconnected from their feelings and have a tendency to be in codependent relationships. They are likely in violent relationships, have almost non-existent boundaries, and are susceptible to human beings-appealing with out regard for themselves. On the other hand, a wholesome fawning reaction is characterised via compromise, energetic listening, equity, and deep compassion for others.

These protection responses are added approximately routinely through the thoughts, giving us no desire in how we react to risky and distressing conditions. These responses are also natural. Identifying those responses as they display up is critical because it will assist you discover strategies to well deal with or paintings thru them and triumph over those conditions in which they're no longer needed. If the mind comes throughout a similar sight, sound, or scent that reminds you of the memories saved, the thoughts will trigger an automatic response whether or not or now not or not the state of affairs is clearly dangerous or now not. Being on immoderate alert is predicted if you have survived a specially unstable occasion. Most instances, the part of the mind liable for shielding you remains on immoderate alert for decades in spite of the truth which you're now constant. It must take a long term for the thoughts to lighten up after a annoying event. This explains why you could sense jumpy, irritable, and continuously in fear regardless of the truth which you realize you're solid now.

Chapter 7: Definition Of Ptsd

PTSD stands for Post-disturbing stress sickness that develops because of an prolonged-time period impact of Trauma on an character. It is also a excessive and extended response to traumatic activities. The occurrence of PTSD is carefully depending at the individual and the form of event professional. It is precipitated by the use of the identical kind of activities that reason Trauma. Examples consist of natural disasters, battle, accidents, abuse, and attack. With PTSD, it's miles not unusual for mind and memories, flashbacks, and visions to stand up in spite of the truth that the danger has exceeded and shows no signs and signs and symptoms of re-going on.

PTSD influences approximately 7 to eight percent of the population, and girls are much more likely to be affected than guys. PTSD disrupts someone's lifestyles. Instead of feeling better as time is going on, the situation degenerates.

Symptoms related to PTSD start internal 3 months after the event. Sometimes the signs and signs and symptoms and symptoms start later. The important signs of PTSD include:

•Reliving the demanding occasion: This takes place through distressing and undesirable recollections, vibrant nightmares, flashbacks, hyper-vigilance, expanded and severe startle reaction, and stressful mind. During moments like those, it's far commonplace to enjoy very disappointed and characteristic intense bodily reactions like coronary coronary heart palpitations or trouble in respiration. Nightmares are a major symptom of submit-stressful stress disease because of the fact the occasion maintains replaying itself. When you entertain the ones in general terrible thoughts, you turn out to be fixated on them. This is called rumination. Rumination is while your mind is stuck on a few component, and your mind constantly evaluates it. These are known as intrusive symptoms and symptoms and signs. They are called intrusive because of the reality they creep into your reality and cognizance. You is probably going approximately your each day sports activities, and then the idea or the memory of the annoying event cuts into your recognition and rattles you.

•Avoiding reminders of a worrying event: They are also known as avoidance signs and symptoms and symptoms and signs. These encompass fending off sports activities activities, humans, places, mind, or feelings that would carry lower back recollections of the worrying occasion. Avoidance symptoms encompass refusing to talk about the event and avoiding situations that might trigger a flood of unwanted memories.

•Symptoms that have an impact on mood and thoughts: Feeling worry, anger, guilt, disgrace, numbness, and infection. An individual could likely blame themselves or others for the superiority of the event. They enjoy changes in temper and feature an impact on. Affect definitely refers to how your look or countenance seems to a person else. They may also reduce themselves off from pals and family. They moreover normally have a tendency to lose interest in every day activities. They are plagued with the useful resource of an disability to don't forget some factors of the event. There are distinguished emotions of guilt and blame. They have a propensity to become detached and estranged from others, giving a opportunity of emotional and intellectual numbness. They moreover generally tend to extend phobias and function first-rate issue focusing.

•Feeling wound up: These signs and symptoms are known as hyperarousal and reactivity symptoms and symptoms and symptoms. This includes having trouble slumbering, concentrating, feeling irritated and irritable, taking reckless dangers, being resultseasily startled, continuously searching out risk, paranoia, and feeling stressful and demanding. To be diagnosed with PTSD, people must meet the necessities set out thru the American intellectual association's diagnostic and statistical guide. According to the criteria

•The person have to have been exposed to loss of life or threatened with the aid of it. They should have a intense harm or professional sexual violence without delay. They have to have witnessed it taking place to a loved one or appearing expert duties.

•The person need to enjoy one or more of all the signs and symptoms and symptoms and signs of PTSD for extra than a month. Just like Trauma, there are bodily signs and symptoms and signs and symptoms that come together with PTSD, which consist of:

1. Sweating, shaking, headaches, dizziness, digestive problems, aches, pains, problem breathing, coronary heart palpitations, and chronic migraine complications. They additionally experience out of manage weight benefit.

2. Trauma can result in a weakened immune device that leaves the person vulnerable to

commonplace infections or a gradual decline in health. There is likewise proof of horrible appetite, regarding overindulging in food or now not consuming sufficient. This also offers to the health issues.

3. Restlessness and sleep disturbance can bring about fatigue and exhaustion.

PTSD motives drastic behavioral adjustments which have an effect on an individual's entire lifestyles. It can purpose issues at art work and, in maximum times, causes an entire breakdown in an man or woman's present relationships. It moreover prevents them from entering into new healthy relationships. The man or woman is vulnerable to emotional outbursts and temper swings, and in most times, they have a propensity to rely closely on alcohol and drugs to manipulate. They also are liable to misusing drugs and self-medicating, which has volatile long-term effects.

It has been established that PTSD influences adults of every genders, kids, and young adults. Children beneath the age of 6 might also furthermore have symptoms and signs and symptoms like bedwetting even after getting to know to use the bathroom, becoming selectively mute, or the entire inability to speak. They tend to come to be clingy and act out the occasion for the duration of playtime.

Children a number of the a long term of 6 and 12 years may not have flashbacks and could now not have hassle remembering the occasion, however in most instances, they will be predisposed to don't forget it in a brilliant order. They furthermore depict or reenact the event via play, pics, and tales. They are liable to having nightmares. They have troubles staying in social situations as they will be predisposed to be withdrawn. They have troubles focusing on paintings and faculty.

Children a few of the a long time of 12 and 18 can also moreover react and feature similar signs and symptoms and signs and symptoms and symptoms and signs to adults. They have a propensity to be disruptive, disrespectful, impulsive, and overly competitive. They are liable to feeling accountable for no longer performing in some other way and might harbor or nurture emotions of revenge, specifically in sexual or physical abuse and forget instances.

Children who have skilled sexual abuse are much more likely to sense fear, sadness, anxiety, and self-isolate. They normally typically tend to have low conceitedness and a low experience of actually in reality worth. They flip to self-harm and adverse behaviors. They are commonly competitive or show uncommon sexual behavior. Some have a tendency to be hypersexual, while others boom a phobia for subjects of sexual nature.

CAUSES

Much like Trauma, PTSD is due to annoying events, which encompass however not constrained to herbal screw ups, attack, army confrontations, civil unrest, conflict, intense accidents, terrorist attacks, rape, and different varieties of abuse. It is likewise because of forget, dropping a cherished one, or receiving a existence-threatening evaluation.

Any or all conditions that motive fear, helplessness, wonder, and terror can cause the improvement of PTSD.

Although it has now not but been determined why a few humans boom PTSD after a stressful experience and others do no longer, some elements boom the danger of developing PTSD. The risk factors consist of the subsequent:

•A essential chance problem that could purpose the development of PTSD is a similarly unexpected and unlucky event that takes place proper now after a worrying occasion, for instance, losing your associate and then your task internal a brief length. Another example is being in a extreme twist of fate and no longer lengthy after being diagnosed with a terminal or life-threatening sickness.

•The loss of a assist tool additionally will increase the threat of growing PTSD. Although it could be difficult to address an individual affected by Trauma, they have to have a legitimate assist tool. A actual useful resource gadget this is constantly there for them will assist them cope and get thru the difficult length.

•The risks boom if there may be a records of intellectual fitness issues or substance abuse.

•Past studies of abuse all through early life should boom the threat of growing PTSD. There is a immoderate possibility that adults who have been abused at some point of their children is probably managing unresolved early life trauma. This makes them quite at risk of PTSD and CPTSD in the end.

•Having horrible bodily fitness earlier than the demanding occasion or enjoy came about or awful fitness because of the occasion. There also are physical and genetic factors that increase the risks of growing PTSD

•Brain Structure: Brain scans have proven that the a part of the mind that permits approach recollections and emotions seems to be quite distinct in people who have PTSD in evaluation to those who do now not have the sickness.

•Response to Stress: Research suggests that the levels of hormones launched in a flight or combat state of affairs are one in every of a kind in people who've the illness.

•Gender: Several studies show that no matter the truth that men are maximum likely to be exposed to and experience violence, women have a much higher hazard of having PTSD.

It is critical to do the subsequent to reduce the possibilities of growing PTSD;

•Have a robust beneficial resource device.

•Develop healthful coping mechanisms.

•Improve your reactivity and functionality to experience accurate and confident about the way you act even as going through hard situations.

Over the years, PTSD has been regarded via a couple of names, in conjunction with shell shock sooner or later of the First World War and fight fatigue after the Second World War. Although PTSD is usually tied to battle and can be on account of the trauma war survivors and veterans undergo, it is not specific to conflict veterans on my own. Trauma and Post-traumatic pressure contamination are related because of the disruptions and changes they motive to the mind chemistry. As already set up, it could take region to all and sundry, regardless of ethnicity, nationality, age, or culture.

PTSD impacts approximately three.Five percent of the united states' population every 365 days. That is ready eight million Americans in a given 12 months. 70 percentage of adults enjoy at least one demanding event of their lifetime. About 20 percent of the folks who experience a worrying occasion will growth PTSD. Studies have installed that an expected 3.6 percentage of American adults over the age of 18 are tormented by PTSD. The signs and symptoms of PTSD are grouped via manner of slight, slight, and immoderate impairment tiers. 36.6 percent of adults sufferers revel in intense impairment. 33.1 percent enjoy mild impairment, and 30.2 percent experience slight impairment. Many PTSD information are focused on adults, however it is essential to phrase that Trauma professional in teens does now not result in PTSD until the thoughts is completely developed in maturity.

An expected 5 percentage of kids revel in PTSD, much like the adults who have this illness, and the signs are categorized in line with impairment ranges. About 1.Five percent enjoy extreme impairment. This ailment is greater commonplace in the past due youngster years. There is a three.7 percentage incidence of the contamination in teens amongst thirteen and 17. The range will increase to 7 percentage with teens most of the a while of 17 and 18.

forty nine percentage of rape patients and 32 percentage of sufferers who revel in extreme physical attack extend this illness. Sixteen.Eight percent of those involved in visitors and railway accidents, 15.Four percent of attack patients, and 14.Three percentage of individuals who experience the demise of a loved one increase this infection. 10.Four percent of parents have kids who have been identified with a life-threatening or terminal sickness. 7.Three percentage of folks who witness the murder or the acute damage of every exclusive person and 3.Eight percentage of folks who experience herbal will be inclined to make bigger PTSD.

Many mental fitness troubles can arise along PTSD. Most people with this disorder are susceptible to one or more of the subsequent co-occurring conditions on the facet of:

•Depression: One in ten people has one depressive sickness every 12 months.

Depression is ubiquitous amongst people who have professional worrying activities. They are 3 to 5 instances much more likely to have a co-going on depressive sickness. The normal fear, unhappiness, and disgrace usually precede whole-blown melancholy. As referred to inside the symptoms, many trauma sufferers emerge as socially withdrawn and have a propensity to isolate themselves.

•Suicidal Ideation: This includes the thoughts and moves targeted towards finishing their lives. Experiencing a demanding event will increase the risk of suicide. The ordinary depressive episodes and absence of potential to manipulate their emotions furthermore make contributions to the elements that sponsor suicidal mind and behavior.

•Anxiety: PTSD and anxiety have very comparable signs and symptoms. PTSD turn out to be categorised as an tension disease. Many of the signs and symptoms which is probably manifested via human beings who have anxiety issues and put up-disturbing strain ailment impair essential biological features. Anxiety due to PTSD will growth agitation and makes it difficult to pay interest.

•Substance Abuse: Research suggests that 46.Four percent of people with PTSD meet the standards for substance abuse infection. PTSD and alcohol use issues are extra carefully associated because of the legality of alcohol. It is less complicated to get get proper of entry to to alcohol than drugs. Research additionally suggests that girls with PTSD are 2.Forty eight percent more likely to misuse alcohol coping than guys with the disease.

In modern-day-day times, the evaluation for this disorder has marginally advanced. There also are more effective treatments for the situation. The treatments cast off and not a whole lot less than reduce the signs and symptoms. Studies have observed that people with this sickness who sought out remedy had symptoms and signs last thirty-six (36) months. Those who did now not are attempting to find treatment had their symptoms and symptoms and symptoms last as long as sixty-4 (sixty 4) months.

In addition, a 3rd of the people that have interaction in the treatment do not enjoy or collect whole symptom removal. Still, there may be a huge discount inside the depth of their symptoms. Long-time period evaluation is superior via manner of prompt remedy, strong assist structures, preventing re-traumatization, immoderate functioning in advance than the onset of the sickness, and the whole absence of various intellectual fitness situations.

ORIGIN OF CPTSD

A new analysis modified into proposed in 1988 through way of Judith Herman that could properly describe the results and signs of prolonged-time period Trauma. She believed that the PTSD analysis did now not cowl the great spectrum of this disorder, the extreme mental and physiological damage that happens with extended and repeated

Trauma. She additionally believed that repeated and prolonged trauma times desired unique treatment interest. According to her, such signs include somatization, that may be a scenario wherein mental symptoms and symptoms and signs and symptoms play out as bodily signs and symptoms. Behavioral issues like impulsivity, self-damaging conduct, and aggressiveness. Cognitive issues like dissociation and continual adjustments in non-public identification. Most times, the ones adjustments are terrible. Interpersonal problems like chaotic and risky relationships and emotional stressful conditions like consistent rage, depression, and chronic anxiety.

Disorders of immoderate strain not otherwise positive (DESNOS) are used to explain CPTSD and its cluster of signs and symptoms and symptoms. CPTSD modified into no longer protected inside the DSM IV and DSM 5 because of the fact area trials indicated that 90percent of human beings met the diagnostic requirements for Post-annoying pressure disease. It have become not brought to the DSM five due to the fact there has been little to no empirical proof to assist the need for a very specific analysis.

Regardless of the arguments suggesting CPTSD symptoms and signs and symptoms constitute a completely particular trauma-related illness and advise extra complex PTSD troubles, there had been no remarkable conclusions.

In some revisions to the put up-traumatic strain disorder diagnosis in the DSM 5, some of the CPTSD signs and symptoms have included uncontrollable anger, impulsivity, emotional difficulties, and put up-stressful strain dissociative subtype. It has been counseled that right studies on the dissociative subtype may also remedy disagreements about making CPTSD a evaluation independently. Suppose people who bevia the dissociative subtype are extra susceptible to expose off somatic, behavioral, cognitive, interpersonal, and emotional signs and symptoms and symptoms and signs and symptoms and signs which have been suggested as the hallmarks of CPTSD. In that case, they will be made a evaluation.

The 11th revision of the World Health Organization's worldwide elegance of illnesses (ICD 11) has a great technique. The signs and symptoms that carry in a PTSD assessment in the ICD eleven are re-experiencing a demanding event, avoidance of thoughts, emotions, sports activities, locations, and people that characteristic a reminder of the stressful event, and chronic hyper-arousal; ordinary and heightened perceptions of and reaction to immediate threats. Individuals are taken into consideration to have CPTSD in the occasion that they meet the ones standards and, similarly, have bad or distorted self-picture, unstable private relationships, and affective or emotional dysregulation.

Although the World health business business enterprise has confirmed this new prognosis of CPTSD, the DSM 5 no matter the reality that insists that the signs and symptoms fall under the post-traumatic pressure sickness necessities and does not warrant a completely new or awesome analysis.

The proponents of CPTSD centered on younger humans trauma, specifically Trauma caused by sexual abuse, neglect, and abandonment. There is great evidence that the duration of disturbing publicity is installed to CPTSD, no matter the truth that such exposure takes place superb in maturity, just like the situation with refugees, trafficked humans, and those trapped in lengthy-term relationships characterised thru way of home abuse or violence. According to Dr. Herman, inside the course of extended-time period traumas, people are held in an prolonged usa of captivity or entrapment emotionally or bodily or emotionally, and bodily. In such conditions, the people are really beneath the manage of their captor or tormentor and cannot free themselves.

DEFINITION OF CPTSD

The abbreviation CPTSD stands for complicated submit-annoying pressure disorder. Many people have heard of and are greater familiar with placed up-stressful stress disease. They usually have a extra complete idea of what it's miles and the manner it gives itself, in particular whilst someone comes home from struggle or is going thru a horrific life-threatening occasion. Complex PTSD is a separate elegance or a subset of PTSD many people are unaware of or acquainted with. Complex PTSD is a highbrow health sickness that comes from experiencing a repeated traumatic occasion or incident over time wherein safety is threatened. Complex PTSD refers to a pervasive and continual set of symptoms and signs and symptoms and signs and symptoms. It stems from extended, repeated, or prolonged-term complex Trauma, which includes sexual, physical, highbrow, sexual abuse, and terrifying activities that upward thrust up numerous times at excessive frequency and intensity.

It commonly manifests in people who've professional lengthy-term younger humans physical and sexual abuse. In a few cases, every horrible conditions get up concurrently, and in others, they may be one-of-a-kind. It additionally tends to expand and then manifests in human beings who have skilled prolonged-term home abuse or intimate associate violence, sufferers and survivors of kidnapping, human trafficking, and refugees. It affects human beings who've had prolonged disturbing testimonies or were in long-time period demanding situations wherein break out grow to be nearly not possible and dangerous. The Trauma associated with complex PTSD is of an interpersonal and invasive nature. It is Trauma inflicted with the useful resource of each distinctive character. It usually occurs inside the context of relationships and is common in families and spousal relationships. It usually consequences from own family individuals and interactions with an awful, unpredictable, psychologically and emotionally disturbed/risky decide, caregiver, or guardian. Siblings, partners, and

141

spouses can also be chargeable for developing this infection.

Complex PTSD in youngsters, teenagers, and children takes area inside a dating. Primarily a dating near the kid. In most conditions, complex PTSD stems from a courting wherein there can be an uneven electricity dynamic. There may be a determine abusing a baby or, in some devastating conditions, a issuer abusing their affected character or a attorney their consumer. These choppy strength dynamics create the proper environment for complicated PTSD. This uneven energy dynamic leads to exploitation with devastating consequences. This Trauma motives the affected to lose their enjoy of safety and consider in others.

There are a whole lot of issues with emotion dysregulation and problems in interpersonal relationships. There is likewise excessive reactivity, along facet reacting with immoderate suggests of anger and a deeply rooted fear of relationships. There is a shift in self-belief; humans with complex publish-traumatic strain illness frequently view themselves as shameful and broken. They frequently resort to self-blame over the occasions that befell to them. In a few times, they have an unreal belief of the perpetrators. They see them as all-powerful and usually will be inclined to harbor thoughts and fantasies of revenge toward them. They have problems with attention and hobby. There are disruptions of their capacity to pay interest and focus, making it difficult for them to talk and interact with other people. Some people with complex positioned up-worrying stress sickness have a dissociative extremely good wherein they may be not continuously in music with what's occurring spherical them.

This isn't always the same as the classical presentation seen with conventional Post-disturbing stress sickness, this is more often than not a fear-primarily based disease. There is lots of tension arousal, avoidance, being on aspect, hyper-vigilance, and exaggerated responses to startling sports. Although there is lots of overlap and similarities among put up-demanding strain illness and complex placed up-stressful pressure illness, some of the issues with emotional dysregulation and relationships veer far from what isn't always unusual in conventional PTSD.

Emotional neglect is every different precursor to complex PTSD. Emotional neglect about about takes severa forms, in conjunction with now not being attentive to the child, calling the child names, and consciously or unconsciously ignoring the kid. For adults, emotional neglect about takes place in emotionally and psychologically abusive (A courting in which there can be no physical fighting however is characterised through hurtful terms, passive-aggressive conduct, and movements) or home violent relationships.

Another scenario is whilst, as children, human beings felt dangerous by unique individuals who have been meant to shield them. They begin to enjoy that nothing approximately themselves is suitable, and in searching for to be brave, they must undergo lots of tedious situations. They had been regularly not reassured in their nicely in reality well worth and judged with insupportable harshness. The harm may also have opened up in innocent situations that even regular visitors may not have located.

Research on complicated post-stressful pressure disease has discovered that emotional neglect inside an outwardly challenge family can be as unfavourable and negative as energetic violence in a low-attaining one.

Research has additionally shown a connection among person bodily fitness troubles and a number of the mental fitness troubles that stem from being raised in abusive and perilous homes. The term unstable does not completely recommend to be physical volatile. It moreover covers being psychologically and emotionally dangerous.

When human beings are diagnosed with complex PTSD, they are given the superior teens occasions survey (ACES). This survey includes ten questions targeted on early youth memories and activities of missing safety in the home. Some of those questions are round physical harm, topics within the domestic environment, alcohol or substance use, incidents of arrests or prison, and having bodily desires met. Your score on this survey is decided by way of using what number of questions you answer affirmatively. This survey proves a strong connection among early adolescence existence reviews and physical health problems later in adulthood. These bodily health problems embody situations like diabetes and fibromyalgia. There is also a link among those early life memories and highbrow health issues like despair and anxiety. How secure you have got been as a infant really impacts your outcomes as an adult to a massive amount. It is critical to be conscious that people revel in Trauma in exceptional methods. Some humans have excessive ACES ratings however do no longer have Complex PTSD. Instead, their signs and signs and symptoms and suffering gift as physical fitness issues in adulthood. Trauma manifests in very unpredictable techniques, and the reactions that accompany it range from one man or woman to the subsequent.

MISDIAGNOSIS

Recent findings have proven that Complex publish-stressful strain infection (CPTSD) is regularly first of all misdiagnosed as Borderline character sickness (BPD). This takes location because of the fact a number of the behaviors and signs exhibited by means of humans with complicated positioned up-traumatic pressure ailment are much like borderline individual ailment.

Although those signs and symptoms are similar, they're no longer the identical. Just as there may be a terrific overlap amongst PTSD and CPTSD, there is a similar overlap amongst borderline persona ailment and complicated positioned up-worrying stress disease. This has confirmed to be a assignment to the intellectual health area as the problem of misdiagnosis is pretty common.

There are a few key variations amongst Borderline character ailment and Complex publish-worrying stress sickness, which embody the following:

Despite the be given as genuine with issues, dating annoying conditions, and strong reactivity, collectively with flare-americaof anger, humans with complicated put up-demanding pressure sickness do now not have the chronic abandonment struggles human beings with Borderline person infection face. They do no longer have a crippling worry of abandonment. Instead, they worry relationships. They do no longer sense relationships are solid areas due to their past reviews. People with borderline character illness have an volatile revel in of identity. Most times, it looks as if they do no longer realize who they are. On the other hand, humans with complex put up-annoying pressure sickness have a distorted enjoy or view of themselves in which they take shipping of as real with they will be broken and shameful however are though aware about who they're.

A borderline individual sickness is one of the maximum distressing and dangerous intellectual fitness illnesses as it has the great price of suicide. The suicidal and self-harming inclinations of borderline man or woman disorder are not not unusual among humans with complicated put up-worrying stress disorder. There can be some risk because of the volume of misery accompanying these worrying activities; it is not a part of the classical presentation of complex publish-traumatic stress sickness.

Borderline character sickness has a more extreme sample, and it cannot be considered a model because there are loads of differences. Both issues have in common that most people with borderline character sickness have skilled full-size early early life trauma. It is a not unusual denominator, but no longer anyone who has borderline character contamination has a facts of young people trauma. On the opportunity hand, that is more normative for people with complex positioned up-stressful stress disorder. They usually have a tendency to have skilled long-term and relatively inescapable trauma.

Emotional disruption within the interpersonal cluster for humans with complex PTSD is characterized by way of mistrust, instability, pain, anger, and devaluing themselves of their relationships. An man or woman with borderline persona disorder will not continuously doubt their relational talents. Someone with Complex submit-traumatic stress contamination, but, will continuously devalue themselves. There is also an entire lot of numbing. This entails feeling a long way off, remote, and rarely in track with their emotions. This makes experience due to the fact relationships are threats to them. They revel in harm and Trauma inside the context of a courting. Therefore, numbing takes place. It is essential to phrase that numbing isn't a healthful reaction or coping mechanism. There also are temper law issues due to the fact there are hundreds of poor temper shifts, mind, self-communicate, self-belief, and study of relationships—those mixed outcomes in temper and anxiety symptoms below the emotional umbrella. A lot of the symptoms and signs and symptoms are relational, with a awful view of self and a distorted view of others inside the context of relationships.

There has been masses of competition about how masses overlap exists amongst borderline persona sickness and complicated submit-disturbing strain sickness. Still, the troubles of abandonment, identification catastrophe, self-belief, and the severity of behaviors like suicide and self-damage feature clear-cut versions some of the onesdisorders.

In addition, many human beings laid low with Complex placed up-annoying stress problems are also misdiagnosed with some of tension and depressive issues. They are known as narcissistic, autistic, bipolar, and codependent in maximum cases. These labels are unfairly and mistakenly given, however complex publish-worrying strain sickness has a very immoderate risk of co-occurring with the ones troubles.

DIFFERENCES BETWEEN PTSD AND CPTSD

•The foremost difference among PTSD and Complex PTSD is the prevalence of stressful events. PTSD develops after the superiority of 1 precise occasion or a chain of annoying sports over a quick period. For example, squaddies who serve in struggle-torn zones and are uncovered to scary things in the path of the conflict are probable to come returned returned domestic traumatized. Subsequently, a immoderate percentage of these returnees can be diagnosed with PTSD primarily based totally on the signs and symptoms and signs and signs and behaviors. On the opposite hand, people who have complicated PTSD have skilled severa traumatic activities or incidents in which their safety or the protection of their loved ones had been threatened. As against the only exceptional event with PTSD, Complex PTSD is because of a chain of sports activities that passed off over time. These testimonies collect to the element that affected people display off signs and symptoms of PTSD.

•Another distinction among Complex PTSD and PTSD is the inescapability and chronic nature of the stressful sports that reason the improvement of CPTSD. This is in opposition to episodic publicity to sports in submit-worrying stress disorder.

•The signs and symptoms and symptoms and symptoms associated with Complex PTSD are very much like that of PTSD, but they range in severity. Symptoms related to complex PTSD are a excellent deal more immoderate than those of PTSD.

•People with complicated post-demanding strain problems have disturbing situations with emotion regulation. They revel in beaten through manner in their emotions. Although this furthermore takes vicinity to people with PTSD, it is not as common.

•The trauma that catalyzes complex PTSD is interpersonal. This consists of excessive abuse and bullying, neglect approximately, abandonment, and sexual abuse from a decide. These sports again and again arise to the extent that the affected character loses their feel of protection.

NOTES

A quick recap of this financial ruin:

Post-disturbing strain sickness takes vicinity at the same time as the signs and consequences of trauma very last longer than essential. It additionally takes area whilst the severity of the signs does now not lessen. It is due to the incidence of a highly distressing occasion like struggle. The signs and symptoms are physical, emotional, and cognitive. It is characterized by way of manner of immoderate nightmares and flashbacks. PTSD impacts a huge kind of humans and is also known as the parent sickness of CPTSD.

Complex placed up-worrying pressure disorder modified into proposed as a evaluation through way of Dr. Judith Herman. She believed that PTSD have end up no longer ok to cover the signs supplied on the equal time as an individual is going via trauma of a complex nature.

This sickness can occur whilst an person reviews repeated worrying activities over an extended duration. This sickness is commonly misdiagnosed as a borderline personality sickness because of the reality they have got very similar diagnostic signs and symptoms.

The primary versions among PTSD and Complex PTSD are located in the frequency, depth, period, and nature of the disturbing event. PTSD develops because of a specific singularly traumatic occasion. Complex PTSD but develops due to a sequence of disturbing occasions that takes place constantly over some time. It is likewise interpersonal. This manner the trauma takes vicinity within a relationship with unbalanced strength dynamics. Usually, a power or authority decide takes gain of this imbalance to take gain of the victim to their gain. A majority of adults with Complex PTSD grew up in emotionally abusive and neglectful homes.

The effects of Complex positioned up-disturbing strain sickness also are immoderate and debilitating. It influences each side of existence. Many human beings with complex post-annoying stress troubles do not have solid or healthful relationships. There is an acute loss of accept as true with, and in most times, folks that have been sufferers normally normally generally tend to grow to be emotionally abusive. They have troubles controlling their feelings and feelings and will be predisposed to typically be on excessive alert.

In a few instances, they do not even specific their feelings. This may be termed dissociative. CPTSD additionally influences physical fitness, and studies have established a strong connection among CPTSD and bodily fitness problems in the end.

EXERCISES

After reading this financial catastrophe, you need to be familiar with the definition, motives, signs and symptoms, and consequences of PTSD. This manner you may with out issues choose out the signs and symptoms and signs of PTSD in yourself or the one which you love.

•This week, pay near hobby for your circle of relatives participants or buddies who've been through a traumatic occasion semi-recently to look if you may spot any of the symptoms of PTSD.

•Think once more at the number one time you heard of complex put up-stressful stress illness and take inventory of the way a great deal your knowledge has grown.

•Get a magazine to be aware your observations.

Chapter 8: Causes Of Cptsd

As formerly mounted, complicated put up-disturbing pressure disease is due to prolonged and repeated disturbing activities and situations wherein the victim feels helpless, and break out is shape of not possible. These disturbing stories are created in conditions in which the connection has choppy and unequal power dynamics. In maximum times, this trauma takes vicinity within the context of a dating. It essentially involves one man or woman inflicting emotional and bodily abuse on some different man or woman. It can end end result from one or a mixture of numerous styles of long time or extended demanding conditions like:

•Kidnapping

•Human trafficking and forceful intercourse trafficking (prostitution earrings and brothels)

•Emotional overlook and abandonment.

•Childhood bodily abuse.

•Childhood sexual abuse.

•Growing up in a violent or chaotic domestic

•Having a mentally sick or addicted discern

•Growing up with an absent parent, each through lack of existence or incarceration

•Domestic abuse and intimate companion violence

•Living in a conflict area or a place with continual civil unrest

After being uncovered to trauma continuously for years on give up, the affected man or woman has an inclination to close down mentally and emotionally. This is executed as a technique of self-protection and protection from pain and misery as a consequence of the situation.

Continuous publicity to traumatic situations is a clean danger aspect for developing complex publish-traumatic stress illness. Still, brilliant specific factors boom the opportunities of developing this disorder, including:

•A facts of depression or tension or both; Thesesituations could make anybody more prone to developing Complex located up-annoying strain sickness. Some of the symptoms and signs and symptoms of this disease are depressive and anxiety-triggered episodes.

•A lack of wholesome and supportive relationships also may be a danger element. When human beings do now not have a aid tool, they experience lonely and remoted and function a profound loss of want. An person who has skilled prolonged trauma without a proper manual gadget also can increase complicated submit-annoying pressure disease.

•Although adults enjoy this sickness, youngsters who're continuously exposed to repeated trauma have a immoderate threat of developing it too. They are very susceptible. Most children who have complex post-traumatic pressure contamination have had early research with abuse-related trauma. This makes the body and minds exceptionally liable to this sickness. According to the countrywide infant traumatic stress network, exposure to repeated trauma at an early age interferes with a infant's improvement. It gives them a distorted self-photograph or enjoy of self. This may be very commonplace among children because they will be but developing attachments, relationships, and coping talents. Children also are extra without difficulty trapped in abusive situations due to the truth they can't completely defend themselves.

•Adults, mainly women in abusive relationships, generally have a propensity to expand this disease. Many go through home violence or intimate accomplice violence for an prolonged period. Most times, they fall into the situation of traumatic bonding. This is an dangerous scenario wherein your partner alternates among moments of pure love and torment; the moments of respite in among are never sufficient for them to understand that they want to move away that scenario.

Also, maximum of these girls commonly generally tend to have distorted snap shots in their partners and blame themselves for his or her relationships.

Abusive and emotionally manipulative conditions like those generally usually have a tendency to growth the risk of developing Complex placed up-disturbing strain illness.

SIGNS AND SYMPTOMS OF CPTSD

The following are symptoms and signs and symptoms and signs and symptoms that announce the presence of complicated PTSD

•The avoidance of activities, people, and locations related or related to the trauma

•Deliberate avoidance of thoughts, feelings, and conversation related to the trauma

•The affected character is constantly in a country of hyper-arousal and vigilance. They also have severe startle reactions. These reactions may additionally appear like an over-exaggeration or overreaction to others.

There is a experience of being risky and a consistent apprehension that some issue terrible will seem. This normally consists of a sudden fall from grace, inclusive of humiliation and being denied get right of entry to to whatever great or kind. They are typically alert due to the fact they trust that the incidence of such an event may be the quit in their lives. Despite reassurance and the use of commonplace feel via others, they may be now not in reality glad.

•They will be inclined to have habitual nightmares about the worrying occasion. They additionally experiencesleep, cold sweats, and normal restlessness.

•They also experience intrusive and undesirable memories at a few stage inside the day. This involves random images of the event or terrifying mind invading your thoughts at the same time as doing all your each day sports. Sometimes, those recollections are so top notch they will be debilitating.

•Another signal is the lack of potential to loosen up. A lot of people who've this sickness are usually disturbing. They have issues being touched in some regions of the frame. Although meditation, breathing physical sports, and yoga are beneficial, those sports sports generally do now not preserve any enchantment to them.

•It is more not unusual to have emotional flashbacks. This lacks the visible abilities of the flashbacks which may be commonplace in placed up-demanding pressure disease. Emotional flashbacks are the influx of vibrant feelings from the time of the stressful revel in. These flashbacks are enough to carry a fresh wave of pain. They also can be as debilitating as intrusive memories and thoughts.

•Difficulties with interest, reminiscence, and recognition; These problems have an effect on many people, but they'll be traditional symptoms which have an effect on people with complicated put up-traumatic strain sickness. When a toddler is exposed to these worrying situations, they regularly have problems with analyzing, focusing, or simply being nevertheless. These trends are also visible in adults due to being shamed as a infant. This consequences in greater shame whilst suffering with those equal learning problems. Also, recognize that teenagers traumas have an impact on a person emotionally and result in thoughts modifications which have an impact on memory, popularity, and studying procedures. These troubles are commonplace for a person who has expert trauma. This symptom is commonly flawed for interest deficit disease (ADD) or interest deficit hyper infection (ADHD).

•Numbing and spacing out at the same time as making selections or discussing emotions. This is an characteristic of dysregulation. There is emotion dysregulation, which doubles as an impact of this ailment. There is also mind and apprehensive device dysregulation, which develops due to trauma. It is an damage to everyday functioning that is very primary but can be healed. It additionally develops as a protecting mechanism to shield a infant's developing mind from the capacity damage of excessive trauma. The toddler has a tendency to shut down interest of some thing that is too terrible to stand. This coping mechanism is top notch for a child however turns into difficult as it persists in maturity. An adult with this coping mechanism tends to close down mentally or freeze up in situations that require rapid reaction. Research shows that those freeze-u.S.A.Or lack of rational idea in disturbing situations factor to dysregulation. It can be seen in MRIs and thoughts scans that the thoughts waves end up discordant at the same time as you're pressured.

•Trouble regulating immoderate feelings; Most people who've this illness have surprising and irrelevant outbursts of negative emotions, inclusive of anger and sadness. It is critical to be aware that complicated placed up-traumatic stress ailment is not the handiest motive human beings are emotionally dysregulated. Still, it's miles established for people who have the sickness. This takes vicinity even as they may be brought on via grievance, being judged harshly, rejection, feeling overlooked, undue strain or pressure from paintings, feeling omitted or burdened out.

•People who are traumatized as kids, even as they may be pressured as grown-ups, have a stylish response to strain within the right the front cortex of the mind, in which feelings are activated. The left the the front cortex that handles reasoning and rational concept is not activated along it. When the left thing is suppressed, emotions run unchecked, and there is lots of overreaction, particularly with anger, delight, and disappointment. In maximum instances, after an person critiques these moments of immoderate emotions, they plummet into numbness. This state of affairs can show unreasonable and scary in your family.

•Another symptom of this illness is a consistent conflict in your interpersonal relationships, typically with circle of relatives, pals, and coworkers. Emotional dysregulation plays a big function right proper here because it aggravates any war situation. These problems with interpersonal relationships cease result from growing up inside the disturbing situations that cause this disorder. It also can cease result from growing up without proper steerage characterized through a scarcity of love, forget, or being punished closely for little mistakes. There is also a chronic distrust which results in a existence entire of numerous loss and fear that they will constantly break their relationships.

•Social anxiety is some different sign which you have complex put up-stressful pressure infection. This manifests inside the vulnerability you enjoy at the same time as round different people. Another pointer to social anxiety is whilst you begin to keep away from social sports, engagements, and gatherings because of the truth people are triggering. You recognise you have social anxiety whilst you consciously avoid going out, turning into a member of agencies, assembly up with pals, or perhaps making new buddies. Sometimes, you can do these items but hold the alternative individual or human beings at arm's period. Social anxiety is a high motive human beings with this ailment enjoy by myself and remoted despite the fact that they'll be with different people or whilst their loved ones try their hardest to attain out to them and show them, love. Social tension is a few one-of-a-kind reason why many people who have experienced trauma opt to isolate themselves. They see being alone due to the fact the handiest way to be at peace. In addition to tension, there's a deeply rooted paranoia. There is a fake expectation that human beings might be damaging therefore seeking out for possibilities to humiliate them.

•The pressure related to getting near people or commencing new connections can be this form of large burden for humans with this sickness that they occasionally have a propensity to live in very lousy and poisonous relationships. Most people in this example want to go away such situations, but the idea of leaving the bad dating and the strain of starting a new one is placed with the useful resource of panic and despair that makes them live positioned. Many humans who've this ailment get proper proper into a mood in which they accomplice bliss with in no manner having to are to be had touch with a few different person.

•Another signal and symptom of having complex submit-demanding stress disorder is the enchantment to unavailable, abusive, risky, or disruptive humans. If that is you, it does no longer mean which you are a horrific individual, however your capability to proper away determine who is a sincere person has been eroded via way of dysregulation. It is a vicious cycle due to the fact the idea of forming new connections reasons pressure, and stress reasons dysregulation.

Dysregulation motives terrible judgment, which motives you to be related to people who do not have your extraordinary interest. This is how trauma receives handed down through generations. You may moreover look again for your options and be difficult on your self, however you want to recall that this grow to be on occasion a preference you made. Remember that this disorder can purpose such unconsciousness and dysregulation. You might not recognize that there can be a few factor wrong until you are deep into the connection.

•Depression, anxiety, and a slew of other intellectual fitness issues are telltale signs of the lifestyles of complex publish-disturbing pressure ailment. Depression and tension are intellectual health situations carefully related to complicated positioned up-stressful stress sickness and publish-annoying pressure ailment.

•The use of alcohol, drugs, and cigarettes in an addictive way; The use of those materials enables modify and soothe extreme emotional outbursts quick time period however outcomes in even more lengthy-time period emotional dysregulation. There is a excessive opportunity of addiction and substance abuse.

•Another sign is being obese or continual overeating. Early early life trauma can alter your metabolism and the hormones chargeable for urge for meals and craving. This explains why many people have little manipulate whilst spherical certain meals and do now not prevent eating even if they are complete. Binge eating is likewise a signal of this illness.

•Recurrent and unexplained physical ailments are some other signal of complicated put up-disturbing pressure disease; These ought to encompass migraines, belly troubles, low immunity, persistent again ache, nausea, and fibromyalgia signs. There is also a connection between this sickness and maximum cancers, diabetes, and coronary coronary heart troubles. Having your bodily fitness affected significantly by way of this trauma is enough motive to are on the lookout for for professional highbrow fitness care.

•Dissociation is some other symptom of this sickness, in which human beings damage a long way from themselves or their reality. They aren't observed in a scenario. This is also termed a disruption in hobby and interest. It is plain to at least one-of-a-type humans that they are no longer present, or they seize themselves and ask for a replay of what they not noted—having other humans see them as immodest or truly distracted. This can be wrong for Attention Deficit Disorder (ADD). It makes studying, paintings, and interpersonal relationships a trouble. Even conversations can be tough to study. Because of this, maximum people with this sickness will be predisposed to experience on my own and disconnected from exclusive people. They experience separated from others. This feeling is regular for individuals who have been abused and ignored in adolescence. You need to apprehend that this isn't your fault, and you may heal truely from this trauma. Neurological research on the relationship among trauma and interest primary normal overall performance and interest on people who've persisted trauma shows that trauma in all its workplace paintings disrupts the eye techniques.

•Amnesia is a few one-of-a-kind sign of complex submit-stressful strain illness. Amnesia is a blockage of memory in which an man or woman can not undergo in mind sports across the trauma. There is likewise dissociative amnesia which happens at some stage within the time of the trauma. The person actually can't preserve in thoughts the trauma; this is horrible because of the reality specific people doubt the authenticity of the survivor's annoying revel in and its outcomes. It is critical to phrase that reputation, interest, and reminiscence are related to number one worrying device techniques. EFFECTS OF CPTSD

• Traumatic bonding: This is a situation in which you bond with someone you care for and love. These individuals you bond with are usually riddled with instabilities and inconsistency. They alternate between periods of being very wonderful and periods of being very terrible and torturous. It is hard for you to pull away long enough to decide that you need to get out of the relationship. It also keeps you enduring these alternating periods, although you know that the situation is wrong and potentially harmful. If you have gone through or experienced traumatic bonding, you will most likely have a hard time forming secure attachments and healthy relationships. These individuals tend to be codependent, dominating, impulsive, emotionally abusive, and make terrible relationship decisions. There is a high possibility of trust issues; you might distrust your partner. When you do not have a secure attachment, you begin to behave negatively in the relationship, affecting both of you. This affects all relationships, including family, friendships, romantic relationships, and relationships with your coworkers.

• Emotional hiding: This is another effect of complex PTSD. This is a situation in which you hide your emotions. You do not show any emotions, including love, nervousness, anger, joy, or hatred. You also tend to avoid, be defensive, and internalize your genuine feelings.

• Emotional dysregulation and hypersensitivity: These are also common effects of complex PTSD. Emotional dysregulation is when you cannot control or regulate your emotions or what you are feeling. Poor emotion regulation often results in angry outbursts or long periods of persistent sadness.

• Hypersensitivity goes hand in hand with hypervigilance. This is a situation where you are constantly alert and ready for any danger, although there is no cause for alarm. This comes from a place of vulnerability caused by previous hurtful situations.

• Many people who have this disorder suffer from fragile and almost non-existent self-esteem. They also have attachment disorders due to the distrust they develop on the heels of the traumatic experiences.

• They suffer from social anxiety: They feel disconnected from people and tend to self-isolate. They are riddled with feelings of guilt, shame, and worthlessness. They generally have very poor and distorted self-images.

• The complex post-traumatic stress disorder symptoms show the damaging and disruptive effects of long-term and repetitive trauma.

BEHAVIOR ASSOCIATED WITH CPTSD

Some of the behaviors of people who have complex post-traumatic stress disorder include the following: some of the behaviors could double as symptoms and also effects of this disorder. The behaviors are things people struggling with this disorder would do that indicate a very high level of distress.

• Substance use and abuse: One really common behavior is substance abuse, which includes consuming alcohol and drugs constantly. In some cases, this behavior is classified as a quality of life interfering behavior and life-threatening behavior. It is a problematic behavior with long-term consequences, but it makes sense given the amount of pain, suffering, and triggers they endure daily. Self-medicating, binge drinking and drug abuse are coping mechanisms to numb the pain. This behavior needs to be appropriately and quickly addressed as it most often leads to dependence and impairment.

• Self-harming behavior: It has been established that there is an overlap in the presentation of borderline personality disorder and complex post-traumatic stress disorder that could result in a misdiagnosis. Self-harming behavior is one of the overlapping similarities between borderline personality disorder and complex post-traumatic stress disorder. This behavior works the same way for people who have a borderline personality disorder. It is used as a coping mechanism to alleviate emotional distress and pain. In cases where the affected individual is numbing or detached, self-harm serves as a way to feel. It could be termed as a self-medication strategy like the use of drugs and alcohol. The problem with self-harm is that it leaves visible scars from cutting, whipping, or other harmful practices. Given how the body works when you hurt yourself, it releases pain-relieving chemicals that tend to be slightly addictive.

• Pleasing others: They have a deeply rooted need to be compliant and please others regardless of personal discomfort. This might be a bit of a contradiction to the feeling of being detached. Suppose an affected individual is high functioning enough to be out and about in society, and they feel unsafe with interpersonal interactions. In that case, they will resort to doing anything to reduce the chances of potential harm. This results in a pattern of people-pleasing to remain in their good graces no matter what. This behavior is detrimental to the affected individual because there may be no personal boundaries or limits.

FIVE UNIQUE CPTSD FEATURES

According to Pete Walker, there are specific features peculiar to Complex post-traumatic stress disorder:

•   Emotional Flashbacks: This particular feature doubles as a symptom and an effect of complex post-traumatic stress disorder. They are the most noticeable feature of complex post-traumatic stress disorder. It is very similar to the flashbacks associated with post-traumatic stress disorder, but emotional flashbacks do not have the same visual and auditory elements that the usual flashbacks have. Flashbacks as a whole can be quite disorienting and terrifying. As the name implies, they are emotions that take you back to how you felt when this traumatic event took place. In most cases, these emotional flashbacks can be so overwhelming. These flashbacks are triggered by a situation that reminds you of the traumatic experience that you experienced, especially if the event occurred during childhood. When children are abused or neglected, they have limited options because they cannot defend themselves. They tend to freeze or dissociate to deal with the situation as a defensive response. As adults, when these individuals are triggered, they are taken back to when the feeling of helplessness, despair, fear, and being trapped was prevalent. In some cases, these feelings come back without any associated memories because the trauma happened before they could speak. Pete Walker defines emotional flashbacks as sudden and prolonged regressions to the frightening events of childhood, especially the feelings of being neglected, abandoned, and abused. Feelings that commonly accompany these flashbacks include rage, anger, sorrow, shame, alienation, grief, and depression, and it serves as an unnecessary trigger for the fight or flight instinct. Adults who went through traumatizing abandonments as children are susceptible to painful emotional flashbacks. Although they are in a different time, the feelings of distress and powerlessness can be as overpowering as they were when the original traumatic event occurred. The problem with emotional flashbacks is that individuals that experience these flashbacks are riddled with feelings of loneliness and shame for having these intense episodes. They feel alienated and believe that they are not normal. It is important to note that these episodes are normal for someone deeply affected by complex trauma or who has complex post-traumatic stress disorder. They are a normal consequence of growing up in an abnormal environment, and none of it is your fault. When you have an emotional flashback, it is very common to think that the feelings you experience are related to what is happening around you in the present time or whoever you are with is making you feel that way. Often, other people view these reactions as irrational, making the feeling worse. Emotional flashbacks might feel like sadness, irritability, the feeling of stillness, or the urgent need to get away from everything and everyone. It can also feel like constant agitation. When you are unaware that an emotional flashback is happening and take conscious measures to re-regulate, it tends to escalate pretty quickly.

Although these flashbacks are problematic when you are not properly aware or conscious of them, they can be used as an opportunity to grieve. They are opportunities to properly express and release old feelings of fear, rage, hurt, and abandonment. They serve as a means to validate your experiences and heal the still open wounds from the abuse, abandonment, and neglect.

They are also a pointer to unmet developmental needs and are motivated to meet them. Emotional flashbacks still work the same way for people who did not suffer childhood abuse, neglect, and abandonment.

The feelings are major of intense fear of being unable to escape and sometimes rage at being trapped in a situation they had no control over.